CLASSIC BIBLE STORIES

JESUS:
The Road of Courage

—◆—

MARK:
The Youngest Disciple

TITAN BOOKS

CLASSIC BIBLE STORIES
JESUS: THE ROAD OF COURAGE
MARK: THE YOUNGEST DISCIPLE

ISBN: 9781848565258

Published by Titan Books, a division of Titan Publishing Group Ltd.
144 Southwark Street, London, SE1 0UP

All *Eagle* material © Colin Frewin and Associates Ltd. 2010.
All rights reserved. No portion of this book may
be reproduced or transmitted in any form or by any means, without the express
written permission of the publisher.

Grateful thanks to Des Shaw and Carl Alexander for their support and
assistance in the production of this book.

A CIP catalogue record for this title is available from the British Library.

This edition first published: March 2010

1 3 5 7 9 10 8 6 4 2

Cover Illustrations by Frank Hampson.

Printed in China.

What did you think of this book? We love to hear from our readers. Please email
us at: **readerfeedback@titanemail.com**, or write to us at the above address.

To receive advance information, news, competitions and exclusive Titan
offers online, please register as a member by clicking the "sign up" button
on our website: **www.titanbooks.com**

Much of the comic strip material used by Titan in this edition is exceedingly rare. As such,
we hope that readers appreciate that the quality of reproduction achievable can vary.

JESUS

THE ROAD
OF COURAGE

Written By
Marcus Morris

Drawn by
Frank Hampson

ROME

MISTRESS OF THE WESTERN WORLD, 2,000 YEARS AGO.

MAKE WAY— MAKE WAY THERE!

IN THE NAME OF CAESAR, MAKE WAY!

ORDERS FROM CAESAR GO OUT TO THE WHOLE EMPIRE...

I DEMAND PASSAGE, IN THE NAME OF GREAT CAESAR!

THERE'S YOUR DESTINATION— JOPPA, PORT FOR JUDAEA.

TAKE ME TO HEROD, KING OF JUDAEA!

FRANK HAMPSON

GREETINGS, YOUR MAJESTY...

I BRING ORDERS FROM THE EMPEROR— GREAT CAESAR.

H'M— SO CAESAR WANTS A CENSUS, DOES HE?

GUARD COMMANDER! SEND PATROLS INTO THE CITY, AND DOUBLE THE GUARD ON THE PALACE...

YES, SIR!

CAESAR HAS ORDERED A CENSUS— IN JUDAEA, THAT MEANS BLOODSHED!

Fearing heavier taxation, the Jews of Jerusalem riot when Caesar orders a census. A Roman soldier seizes Bar-Abbas, a young Jew.

HEY!

...SO I SLIPPED OUT OF MY COAT, FATHER, AND GOT AWAY—BUT HE KNOWS MY NAME IS BAR-ABBAS.

H'M—YOU'D BEST GO TO YOUR AUNT IN NAZARETH UNTIL THIS BLOWS OVER.

AND SO...

ON THE OUTSKIRTS OF NAZARETH...

OUT OF THE WAY, BOY!

ROMAN BULLIES!

Fuming, Bar-Abbas follows the Roman patrol into Nazareth, and hears a proclamation read . . .

...AND EACH MAN MUST GO WITH HIS FAMILY TO HIS HOME TOWN TO BE COUNTED.

DOWN WITH ROME!

BREAK IT UP!

GO BACK TO YOUR HOMES!

HEY— YOU! STOP!

NOT ME—I'M OFF...

THAT'S THE KID WHO GAVE ME THE SLIP IN JERUSALEM.

GET HIM!

TRAPPED! I'LL HAVE TO TRY THAT OPEN DOOR...

OPEN— IN THE NAME OF ROME!

EASY, YOUNG FELLOW! WHAT'S THE HURRY?

PLEASE HELP ME, SIR—THE ROMANS ARE AFTER ME!

YOU'D BETTER HIDE HERE UNTIL IT'S DARK. THEN YOU CAN GO TO YOUR AUNT'S HOUSE.

THAT EVENING...

QUIET— THERE'S SOMEONE AT THE DOOR! GET UNDER MY WORKBENCH...

JOSEPH BAR-JACOB, YOU AND YOUR HOUSEHOLD ARE IN THE PARTY TO GO TO BETHLEHEM TOMORROW FOR THE CENSUS. REPORT IN THE MARKET-PLACE AT DAWN!

BUT WE CAN'T GO—MY WIFE IS EXPECTING A BABY...

THAT MAKES NO DIFFERENCE.

OH, MARY, YOU'RE BACK—I WAS JUST TELLING...

IT'S ALL RIGHT, JOSEPH—WE'LL GO...

Fearing heavier taxation, the Jews of Jerusalem riot when Caesar orders a census. A Roman soldier seizes young Bar-Abbas, but he escapes and takes refuge in Joseph Bar-Jacob's carpenter's shop at Nazareth . . .

HAS HE GONE? CAN I COME OUT NOW?

I'D LIKE THE BABY TO BE BORN IN BETHLEHEM—IT'S GREAT KING DAVID'S BIRTHPLACE.

WHOEVER'S THIS?

HIS NAME IS BAR-ABBAS, AND HE'S HIDING FROM THE ROMANS...

NAZARETH ISN'T REALLY SAFE FOR YOU, BOY—BUT WE COULD TAKE YOU WITH US TO BETHLEHEM.

THEN I COULD GO ON TO MY UNCLE IN BEERSHEBA. THANK YOU, SIR!

SIX DAYS LATER...

BETHLEHEM IS WHERE THE PROPHETS SAY OUR CHRIST WILL BE BORN.

THE MAN WHO'S GOING TO THROW THE ROMANS OUT OF THE COUNTRY? IS HE EVER COMING?

HIS COMING MAY BE CLOSER THAN YOU THINK.

OH, GOOD! I'LL FIGHT FOR HIM—I WANT TO SPEND MY LIFE FIGHTING THE ROMANS.

LISTEN!

BETHLEHEM IN SIGHT!

BUT BETHLEHEM IS CROWDED...

THERE'S NO ROOM IN THE INN—WE'RE FULL RIGHT UP!

WHAT ARE WE GOING TO DO, THEN?

SLEEP IN THE FIELDS, FOR ALL I CARE!

BUT, SIR...

I'VE TOLD YOU, WE'RE FULL UP. NOW STOP WASTING MY TIME, AND CLEAR OFF!

Palestine, nearly 2,000 years ago. Bar-Abbas, a boy of 15 on his way to Beersheba, has travelled to Bethlehem with Joseph and Mary, who have to go there for a census ordered by the Roman Emperor. They find Bethlehem crowded, and are told there is no room for them in the inn . . .

WE *MUST* FIND SHELTER—MY WIFE'S EXPECTING A BABY! WHAT?

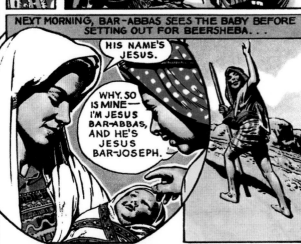

WHY DIDN'T YOU SAY SO BEFORE? WE'LL SQUEEZE YOU IN SOMEWHERE...

IT'LL HAVE TO BE THE STABLE, BUT YOU'LL FIND PLENTY OF GOOD WARM STRAW THERE.

THAT NIGHT... WHATEVER'S GOING ON?

MARY'S BABY HAS BEEN BORN!

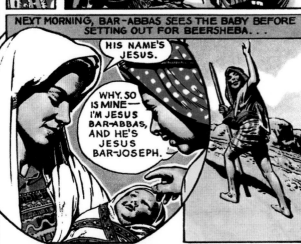

NEXT MORNING, BAR-ABBAS *SEES* THE BABY BEFORE SETTING OUT FOR BEERSHEBA...

HIS NAME'S JESUS.

WHY, SO IS MINE— I'M JESUS BAR-ABBAS, AND HE'S JESUS BAR-JOSEPH.

SOME TIME LATER, IN JERUSALEM, KING HEROD ENDS A WORRYING INTERVIEW...

THAT IS AGREED, THEN, GENTLEMEN— WHICHEVER OF US HEARS ANYTHING WILL INFORM THE OTHERS...

AND NOW YOU MUST BE TIRED AFTER YOUR LONG JOURNEY FROM THE EAST. MY SERVANTS HAVE PREPARED QUARTERS FOR YOU...

THANK YOU, YOUR MAJESTY.

HEAVEN PRESERVE ME FROM ASTROLOGERS! THEY SEE A NEW STAR IN THE SKY, DECIDE IT MEANS THE BIRTH OF SOME GREAT MAN....

AND THAT THIS CHILD IS TO GROW UP TO SEIZE *YOUR* THRONE AND BECOME KING IN *YOUR* PLACE!

AND THEY ASK *ME* WHERE THIS USURPER HAS BEEN BORN! HERE, HIGH PRIEST— *YOU* SHOULD KNOW...

WHERE *HAS* THIS CHILD BEEN BORN?

THE OBVIOUS PLACE, YOUR MAJESTY, WOULD SEEM TO BE BETHLEHEM!

Jesus is born at Bethlehem. A little later, three astrologers arrive in Jerusalem with a story of having seen, in the stars, the birth of a new king of the Jews. Herod, the reigning Jewish King, is furiously angry at this news; he is told by the High Priest that the new King's birthplace must be the town of Bethlehem...

SO YOU THINK IT'S BETHLEHEM, DO YOU? WHY?

IT'S OBVIOUS, YOUR MAJESTY— OUR PROPHETS FORECAST THAT THE CHRIST WILL BE BORN THERE.

THE CHRIST? THAT SILLY DREAM THE PEOPLE HAVE OF A MAN SENT BY GOD TO RESCUE THEM FROM ROME?

AND YET, IF THE PEOPLE BELIEVE THAT THE CHRIST HAS BEEN BORN, THERE COULD BE TROUBLE. I MUST FIND OUT MORE. . .

FETCH THOSE ASTROLOGERS TO MY PRIVATE ROOM!

THE PLACE MAY BE BETHLEHEM— GO AND LOOK THERE, AND LET ME KNOW IF YOU FIND ANYTHING. I WOULD LIKE TO PAY MY RESPECTS TO MY—ER—SUCCESSOR.

OF COURSE, YOUR MAJESTY!

FRANK HAMPSON

DO WE LET HIM KNOW?

NEVER!

I AGREE— HE'S NOT TO BE TRUSTED!

SOME DAYS LATER...

YOUR MAJESTY — THOSE ASTROLOGERS SHOULD HAVE RETURNED BY NOW. I THINK *THEY'RE NOT COMING BACK!*

THEN I MUST PROTECT MY THRONE, AND THAT MEANS...

GUARD COMMANDER!

TAKE A DETACHMENT TO BETHLEHEM, COLLECT EVERY BOY OF TWO AND UNDER, *AND KILL THEM ALL!*

NO, SIR!

WHAT?

YOU *DARE* TO DISOBEY YOUR KING?

Jesus is born at Bethlehem. When three astrologers reach Jerusalem with a story of having seen in the stars the birth of a new king of the Jews, Herod, anxious to protect his throne, orders his guard commander to have all children of two and under in Bethlehem killed. The Captain refuses . . .

NOT *MY* KING — I AM A *ROMAN* OFFICER COMMANDING YOUR BODYGUARD, BUT I AM NOT A HIRED EXECUTIONER OF BABIES.

PAH!

MORE FOOL YOU! IF THE CHILD LIVES, IT MEANS CIVIL WAR . . .

I'LL PUT MY IDUMEAN MERCENARIES ON THE JOB — *THEY* WON'T OBJECT. THEY DON'T LIKE JEWS . . .

THE COMPANY WILL PARADE AT DAWN FOR A SPECIAL MISSION TO BETHLEHEM . . .

SERGEANT! TAKE THE MEN TO THE ARMOURY TO DRAW EQUIPMENT.

YES, SIR!

ONE HELMET — ONE SWORD — ONE SHIELD — ONE SPEAR . . .

WHAT — NO ARMOUR?

YOU WON'T NEED ARMOUR FOR KILLING JEWISH BABIES!

KILLING BABIES? COR, WHAT A JOB!

AT BETHLEHEM, THAT SAME AFTERNOON . . .

GOODBYE, JOSEPH!

ONE LAST THING, JOSEPH . . .

GOODBYE, SIRS — AND THANK YOU FOR ALL YOUR PRESENTS FOR THE BABY.

HOW LONG ARE YOU STAYING IN THAT HOUSE YOU'VE RENTED HERE?

A WEEK, PERHAPS MORE . . .

I WOULDN'T STAY *TOO* LONG. WHEN HEROD FINDS THAT WE ARE NOT RETURNING TO REPORT, THERE'S NO KNOWING WHAT HE'LL DO!

MARY, GET YOUR THINGS PACKED — WE LEAVE FOR NAZARETH IN THE MORNING.

BUT I THOUGHT WE WERE STAYING!

I'VE CHANGED MY MIND. IT'S — ER — TIME I GOT BACK TO WORK AGAIN . . .

THAT NIGHT . . .

MARY!

MARY! WAKE UP!

GET UP, MARY—WE'VE GOT TO LEAVE *NOW*—NOT IN THE MORNING!

OH, JOSEPH, WHY?

Jesus is born in Bethlehem, where three astrologers visit Him. They tell Joseph not to stay long, because King Herod may try to hurt the baby. Joseph decides to leave the next morning but, that night, he wakens Mary . . .

I'VE HAD A TERRIBLE NIGHTMARE! I DREAMT THAT HEROD WAS KILLING THE BABY. WE'VE GOT TO GO AT ONCE...

AND WE'RE NOT GOING BACK TO NAZARETH—WE'RE GOING TO EGYPT! WE'VE GOT TO GET RIGHT OUT OF THE COUNTRY— THAT'S WHAT THE DREAM MEANT. . .

IF EVER GOD SPOKE TO A MAN IN A DREAM, HE SPOKE TO ME TONIGHT. . .

So Joseph, Mary and Jesus become fugitives in Egypt. They stay there until Herod's death, then return home to Nazareth . . .

ONE DAY, WHEN JESUS IS FIVE. . .

GOODBYE, MOTHER!

DON'T GO FAR! TODAY'S THE SABBATH, THE REST DAY, WHEN WE GO TO THE SYNAGOGUE FOR A SERVICE.

WHY ARE YOU BREAKING THE LAW?

I'M NOT BREAKING THE LAW, SIR.

YOU ARE! WORKING ON THE SABBATH IS AGAINST THE LAW.

I WASN'T WORKING — I WAS MAKING MUD BIRDS. I WAS PLAY. . . *OW!*

DON'T ARGUE WITH ME, BOY! COME ALONG — YOUR PARENTS SHALL HEAR OF THIS. . .

MEANWHILE. . .

WHERE *IS* JESUS? WE SHALL BE LATE FOR THE SYNAGOGUE SERVICE.

THERE HE IS! OH DEAR— I THINK HE'S IN TROUBLE!

Jesus, now twelve years old, is acting the story of David and Jonathan with His school-friends in Nazareth, when one of the boys, Simon, is bitten in the ankle by a snake . . .

LOOK OUT!

WHAT'S HAPPENED TO SIMON?

A SNAKE'S BITTEN ME... OH, OH, I'M GOING TO DIE!

QUICK, SIMON! WHERE DID IT BITE YOU?

HERE, ON MY ANKLE... OH, OH!

COME ON—WE MUST GET HIM HOME!

WHAT'S THE MATTER? WHAT'S HAPPENED TO SIMON?

A SNAKE BIT HIM, AND JESUS SUCKED THE POISON FROM THE WOUND!

JESUS SAVED SIMON'S LIFE!

WE MUST GET HIM TO BED.

HE'S GOING TO BE ALL RIGHT—THANKS TO YOU, JESUS.

SIMON RECOVERS—AND, ONE MORNING...

I'VE BEEN THINKING ABOUT YOUR SAVING MY LIFE, JESUS.

WHAT DO YOU MEAN, SIMON?

I THINK GOD HAS GIVEN ME BACK MY LIFE, SO THAT I CAN DO SOME GREAT THING FOR HIM AND HIS PEOPLE...

BUT WHAT?

THAT'S THE TROUBLE—I DON'T KNOW WHAT.

I CAN TELL YOU WHAT!

WHO ARE YOU?

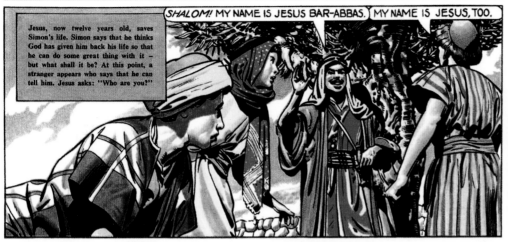

Jesus, now twelve years old, saves Simon's life. Simon says that he thinks God has given him back his life so that he can do some great thing with it — but what shall it be? At this point, a stranger appears who says that he can tell him. Jesus asks: "Who are you?"

SHALOM! MY NAME IS JESUS BAR-ABBAS.

MY NAME IS JESUS, TOO.

THEN GROW UP TO BE A LEADER LIKE OUR NAME-SAKE JOSHUA. HE LED OUR ANCESTORS INTO THIS LAND...

AND THAT'S YOUR JOB—TO HELP US 'ZEALOTS' THROW THE ROMANS OUT...

WHO ARE THE ZEALOTS?

THE NEWLY-FORMED UNDERGROUND MOVEMENT AGAINST ROME. WE'RE ATTACKING THE ARSENAL AT SEPPHORIS TONIGHT!

I HOPE THE ZEALOTS WIN!

I'M GOING TO JOIN THEM WHEN I GROW UP...

That night, at the Roman Arsenal in Sepphoris, the capital of Galilee, as the duty-Sergeant is doing his rounds of the guards...

ALL QUIET, SERGEANT!

JUST AS WELL, WHEN WE'RE UNDER STRENGTH...

I'LL BE ROUND AGAIN IN AN HOUR.

DIE, ROMAN PIG!

THE ROAD OF COURAGE

Jesus, now twelve years old, Simon, and John meet Jesus Bar-Abbas, a member of the Zealots – the underground movement against Rome. Bar-Abbas leaves for Sepphoris, capital city of Galilee, and the same night, the Zealots attack and capture the Roman arsenal situated there . . .

FRANK HAMPSON

THE ROMAN FIGHTING MACHINE IS HURLED AT THE 'ZEALOTS' IN SEPPHORIS ARSENAL...

Jesus, now twelve years old, meets Bar-Abbas, a young man who tells him of the 'Zealots', an underground movement fighting the hated Romans. Bar-Abbas goes off and joins a successful attack on the Roman Arsenal at Sepphoris. The Romans retaliate by sending two legions to put down the Jewish revolt ...

ONLY A FEW ESCAPE AS THE LEGIONS FLOOD IN...

IT'S ALL UP BAR-ABBAS! QUICK — THIS WAY!

SEPPHORIS IS OURS AGAIN, GENERAL.

GOOD. HOW MANY PRISONERS AND HOSTAGES HAVE WE?

ABOUT TWO THOUSAND, SIR

EXCELLENT—SEND OUT TROOPS AND BRING IN ALL THE PEOPLE OF THE SURROUNDING VILLAGES...

THEY SHALL WATCH ROME'S VENGEANCE—THEY SHALL WATCH THE PRISONERS AND HOSTAGES BEING CRUCIFIED!

Jesus is twelve. After the terrible experience of the Sepphoris Executions, comes an event to which he has looked forward eagerly. For the first time, he goes with Joseph and Mary to Jerusalem for the Passover Festival...

DOESN'T THE TEMPLE LOOK WONDERFUL!

YES, I'LL TAKE YOU IN IT WHEN WE'VE PITCHED THIS TENT...

PILGRIMS COME HERE FOR THE PASSOVER FROM ALL OVER THE WORLD...

ONLY JEWS CAN GO BEYOND THIS WALL...

THAT'S THE 'ALTAR OF BURNT OFFERING' AND, BEHIND IT, THE HOLY PLACE ITSELF.

THE PILGRIMS KEEP THE PASSOVER IN THEIR TENTS...

THIS IS THE BREAD OF AFFLICTION WHICH OUR FOREFATHERS ATE IN THE LAND OF EGYPT...

THE NEXT MORNING... WHERE'S JESUS? IT'S TIME TO LEAVE FOR HOME.

HE'LL BE WITH THE OTHER CHILDREN FROM NAZARETH, I EXPECT.

BUT JESUS IS IN THE TEMPLE AGAIN...

THAT MAN'S A ROMAN!

No alien may enter within the barrier and wall around the Temple. Whoever is caught is alone responsible for the death which follows.

STOP THAT MAN! HE'S A ROMAN!

KILL HIM!

FRANK HAMPSON

When Jesus is twelve years old, He goes to Jerusalem for the Passover festival. Jesus is in the Temple, which no alien may enter under pain of death, when a Roman is chased into the Court of Gentiles and seized by an angry mob of Jews . . .

FRANK HAMPSON

THE ROAD OF COURAGE

TRY THE TEMPLE — I SAW A BOY LIKE HIM TALKING TO THE TEACHERS THERE.

OH, THANK YOU... COME ON, JOSEPH!

When Jesus is twelve, He gets left behind in Jerusalem after the Passover festival. Following a day's search, Mary and Joseph still have not found any sign of Him . . .

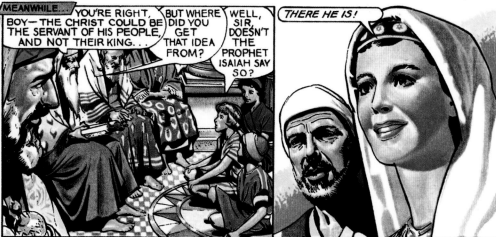

MEANWHILE... YOU'RE RIGHT, BOY — THE CHRIST COULD BE THE SERVANT OF HIS PEOPLE, AND NOT THEIR KING. . .

BUT WHERE DID YOU GET THAT IDEA FROM?

WELL, SIR, DOESN'T THE PROPHET ISAIAH SAY SO?

THERE HE IS!

OH, JESUS, WE'VE BEEN SO WORRIED...

WE'VE BEEN HUNTING EVERYWHERE FOR YOU!

WHY DID YOU HUNT FOR ME? DIDN'T YOU KNOW YOU'D FIND ME IN THE TEMPLE?

BUT, JESUS, YOU MUST. . .

DON'T BE TOO HARD ON HIM, MADAM — YOU'VE GOT A VERY REMARKABLE BOY THERE.

Back home in Nazareth, Jesus works in the carpenter's shop, and takes it over when Joseph dies. Twenty years pass, with the Jews still being ruled by Rome, and then a man appears on the banks of the River Jordan with startling news to impart . . .

GOD'S KINGDOM IS COMING! ARE YOU READY FOR IT?

HURRAY! DOWN WITH ROME!

HOW CAN WE HELP?

CHANGE YOUR WHOLE OUTLOOK...

BE BAPTISED! WASH AWAY YOUR OLD LIFE! MAKE A FRESH START!

ARE YOU SAYING YOU'RE THE CHRIST?

NO, I AM NOT — BUT HE IS COMING!

FRANK HAMPSON

The courtyard of Jesus's home in Nazareth . . .

HEARD ANYTHING OF SIMON LATELY, JESUS?

NO—NOT SINCE HE JOINED THE ZEALOTS.

INTERESTING NEWS ABOUT YOUR COUSIN JOHN, ISN'T IT?

WHAT IS IT? I HAVEN'T HEARD!

HERE COMES EZRA THE PHARISEE.

MORNING, ALL! I'M MAKING UP A PARTY TO VISIT JOHN — YOU'LL COME OF COURSE, JESUS.

WILL SOMEBODY *PLEASE* TELL ME WHAT JOHN'S DOING?

HE'S SET HIMSELF UP AS A PROPHET.

HE SAYS THE KINGDOM IS COMING SOON, AND HE'S BAPTISING PEOPLE IN THE JORDAN.

THEY'VE NICK-NAMED HIM 'JOHN THE BAPTIST'.

So Jesus goes with the Nazareth party to Jordan . . .

GALILEE
NAZARETH o
DECAPOLIS
SAMARIA
JORDAN
PERAEA
JERUSALEM •
JUDAEA

THERE'S JOHN — IN THE RIVER!

I BAPTISE YOU. . .

START A NEW LIFE. . .

THE CHRIST IS COMING SOON. . .

AHEM! EXCUSE ME, JOHN. . .

FRANK HAMPSON

ANOTHER PHARISEE! WHO WARNED YOU THAT GOD IS ANGRY WITH YOU?

I—ER—WELL, *REALLY!*

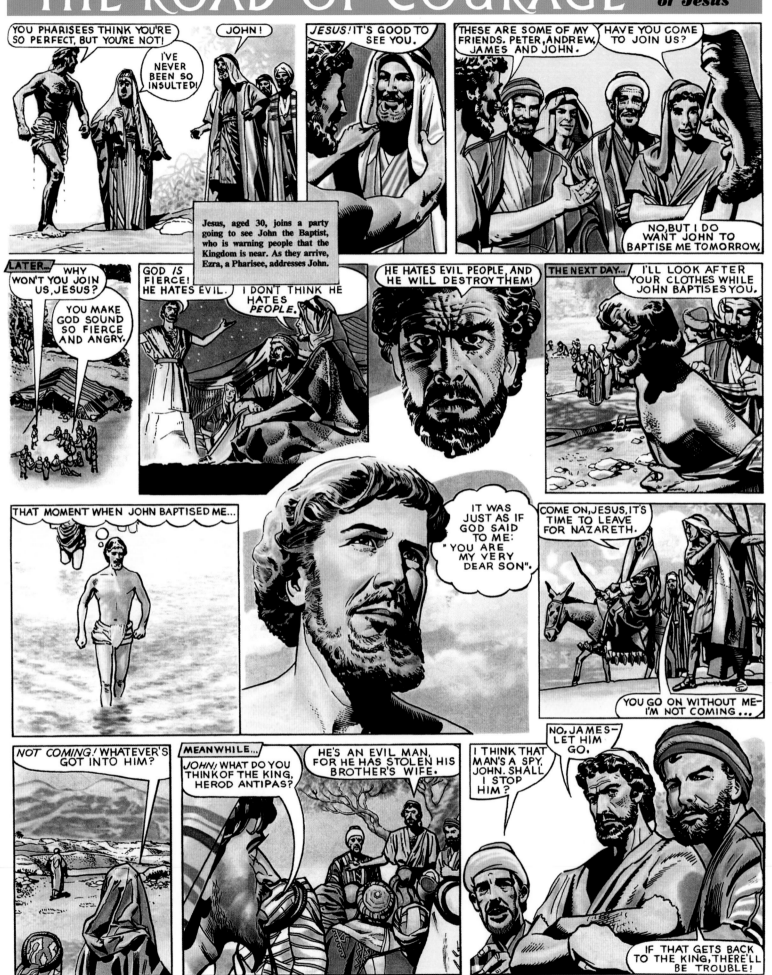

JOHN THE BAPTIST OPENLY CALLS YOU EVIL, SIRE.

YOU HEAR, ANTIPAS? JOHN MUST BE SILENCED!

BUT HE *MAY BE A PROPHET*, HERODIAS — SUCH MEN HAVE POWER...

IF JOHN STARTS A REVOLT, CAESAR WILL DETHRONE *YOU*...

...ALREADY YOUR BROTHER HAS LOST JUDAEA, AND THE ROMAN, PILATE, RULES IN HIS PLACE.

VERY WELL! CAPTAIN, ARREST JOHN!

THE SPY REPORTS TO HEROD ANTIPAS, RULER OF GALILEE AND PERAEA...

COME ON, PROPHET— WE'VE GOT A NICE, COOL CELL WAITING FOR YOU...

WHERE YOU CAN BAPTISE THE LIZARDS!

IF YOU GET ANY WATER! HO-HO!

YOU CAN MOCK *ME*, BUT I WARN YOU— *ONE IS COMING, GREATER THAN I !*

Jesus is baptised by John the Baptist, and immediately goes off on His own, instead of returning to Nazareth. Meanwhile, a spy asks John what he thinks of the king, and John says he is an evil man.

JOHN IS TAKEN TO THE FORTRESS OF MACHAERUS.

SOME WEEKS LATER, IN THE WILDERNESS...

I'LL FIND THAT LAMB, IF IT'S THE LAST THING I DO—OH!

LOOKING FOR THIS?

YES. WHAT ARE YOU DOING OUT HERE?

THINKING THINGS OUT.

OH, WHAT DO YOU THINK YOU ARE — A PROPHET?

A PROPHET? AND HUNGRY? THEN WHY NOT TURN THESE STONES INTO BREAD?

IN A WAY, YES — AND HUNGRY, TOO.

THAT WOULD BE SELFISH.

HA-HA! YOU MEAN YOU THINK YOU COULD? HERE, HAVE SOME REAL BREAD.

THANK YOU.

AND HOW ARE YOU GOING TO GET PEOPLE TO LISTEN TO YOU? YOU'LL NEED TO DO SOMETHING STARTLING, LIKE THROWING YOURSELF OFF THE TOP OF THE TEMPLE ...

TAKE HIM UP TO THE TOP OF THE HILL!

THROW HIM DOWN FROM HERE. THAT'LL CURE HIM FOR GOOD AND ALL!

YOU MEAN — KILL HIM?

Jesus announces in the Synagogue at Nazareth that He has been chosen and inspired by God, but He is shouted down and run out of the Jewish Synagogue. Then a man says that he knows what to do with Him . . .

NO!

LEAVE GO OF ME!

STAND BACK AND LET ME PASS!

SILENT UNTIL NOW, JESUS SUDDENLY SWINGS ROUND AND QUELLS THE MOB WITH HIS DIGNITY AND COURAGE.

ABASHED, THEY WATCH HIM LEAVE NAZARETH.

THAT NIGHT. TELLING PEOPLE GOD SPOKE TO ME AT MY BAPTISM IS THE WRONG WAY—IT UPSETS THEM AND MAKES THEM ANGRY.

I MUST NOT SAY ANYTHING ABOUT IT IN FUTURE.

JESUS TRAVELS EAST, TO THE LAKE OF GALILEE...

WHY, I KNOW THOSE TWO! *HEY, THERE!* CAUGHT ANYTHING?

CAUGHT ANYTHING, PETER?

NO, NOT A THING, JESUS.

DON'T GIVE UP—PUSH OUT INTO DEEP WATER AND TRY AGAIN.

WHAT ABOUT IT, ANDREW?

NO HARM IN TRYING, I SUPPOSE, PETER.

Jesus is thrown out of Nazareth because He claims that God has chosen and inspired Him. Walking by the Lake of Galilee, Jesus recognizes two fishermen whom He knows . . .

FURTHER DOWN THE SHORE...

PETER'S CALLING FOR HELP, JAMES.

HE'S GOT A CATCH, JOHN. QUICK! GET THE OARS OUT..

CAREFUL—THE NET'S BREAKING!

WHEW! WHAT A HAUL!

THAT WAS AMAZING, JESUS. JOIN ME AND CATCH FISH.

NO, I WANT YOU FOUR TO JOIN ME AND CATCH MEN.

DO YOU MEAN YOU'RE TAKING JOHN THE BAPTIST'S PLACE?

SOMETHING LIKE THAT.

THEN LEAD ON! WE'LL FOLLOW YOU.

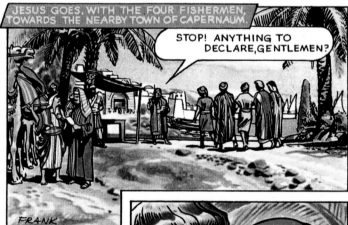

JESUS GOES, WITH THE FOUR FISHERMEN, TOWARDS THE NEARBY TOWN OF CAPERNAUM.

STOP! ANYTHING TO DECLARE, GENTLEMEN?

FRANK HAMPSON

NO, YOU—YOU TRAITOR!

STOP IT, JOHN—COME AWAY!

LOOK AT JESUS! THAT'S A BAD START!

WHAT WILL PEOPLE THINK?

JESUS, ARE YOU MAD? DO YOU KNOW WHO YOU WERE TALKING TO?

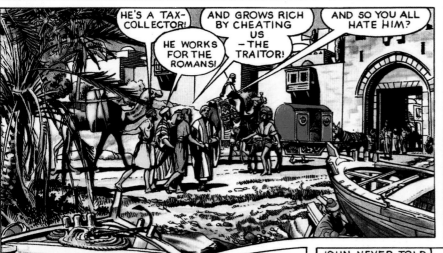

HE'S A TAX-COLLECTOR!

HE WORKS FOR THE ROMANS!

AND GROWS RICH BY CHEATING US —THE TRAITOR!

AND SO YOU ALL HATE HIM?

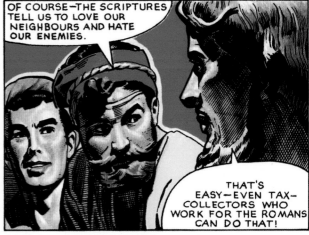

OF COURSE—THE SCRIPTURES TELL US TO LOVE OUR NEIGHBOURS AND HATE OUR ENEMIES.

THAT'S EASY—EVEN TAX-COLLECTORS WHO WORK FOR THE ROMANS CAN DO THAT!

Thrown out of Nazareth for claiming to be inspired by God, Jesus goes to Capernaum, where He meets four friends. When He stops to talk to a customs official, His companions are scandalized . . .

WHAT I TELL YOU IS MORE DIFFICULT: LOVE YOUR ENEMIES TOO.

JOHN NEVER TOLD US THAT.

JOHN IS A VERY GREAT MAN, BUT HE HAS NOT GRASPED THE SECRET OF THE KINGDOM OF HEAVEN.

FRANK HAMPSON

AND WHAT'S THAT?

YOU MUST BE AS PERFECT AS YOUR HEAVENLY FATHER, AND HE CARES FOR ROMANS AND JEWS ALIKE.

Jesus stays in Capernaum with Peter and Andrew. He speaks in the synagogue on the Sabbath and is given an enthusiastic welcome by the people. By doing this, He makes the Scribes (the teachers of the Law) jealous, and upsets the Pharisees – those who keep strictly to the rules of the Law, and so think that they are the only people who know how to serve God properly . . .

WHO IS THAT FELLOW?

A MERE CARPENTER I HEAR.

WONDERFUL SERMON, JESUS!

WHAT A SPEAKER!

HE THINKS HE KNOWS EVERYTHING, DOESN'T HE?

JESUS!

JESUS!

IT'S THAT MAN WHO SAYS AN EVIL SPIRIT HAS TAKEN POSSESSION OF HIM.

YES, YOU—JESUS OF NAZARETH! *I KNOW WHO YOU ARE!*

HE MUST NOT SAY IT . . .

GOD HAS CHOSEN YOU . . .

BE QUIET!

BE QUIET!

WHY DON'T YOU LEAVE ME ALONE? DO YOU WANT TO KILL ME?

Thrown out of Nazareth for claiming to be inspired by God, Jesus determines not to say this again. When a crazed man in Capernaum says the same thing, Jesus orders him to be quiet . . .

STOP TORTURING YOURSELF. GET RID OF FEAR...

DRIVE IT OUT— NOW!

HE'S ALL RIGHT! JESUS HAS CURED HIM!

I'VE NEVER SEEN ANYTHING LIKE IT!

LATER

HE'S DONE IT AGAIN! PETER'S MOTHER-IN-LAW HAD A FEVER, AND JESUS CURED HER!

JESUS, COME OUT AND HELP US!

A CROWD COLLECTS OUTSIDE PETER'S HOUSE.

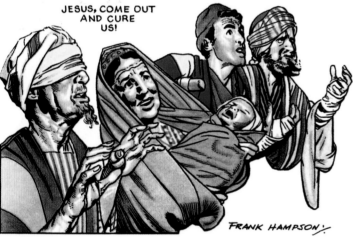

JESUS, COME OUT AND CURE US!

FRANK HAMPSON

WHY DOESN'T HE GO OUT? HE'S MISSING A GREAT CHANCE.

CURING PEOPLE WON'T WIN MEN'S LOYALTY, BUT IT WILL TEMPT ME TO THINK IT DOES.

BUT THOSE PEOPLE NEED YOUR HELP.

AND THAT'S WHY I'M GOING OUT TO THEM. COME ON!

Jesus cures many of the gathered crowd; then, the next morning . . .

ANDREW, ANDREW!

WHAT'S THE MATTER?

IT'S JESUS. I CAN'T FIND HIM ANYWHERE, ANDREW — HE'S DISAPPEARED!

THE ROAD OF COURAGE

FRANK HAMPSON.

A NICE LOT OF BOOTY!

YES, BAR-ABBAS, AND A NICE RICH TAX-COLLECTOR!

NOW THEN, YOU! WHERE'S YOUR MONEY?

The Pharisees accuse Jesus of blasphemy. Bar-Abbas sends Simon to persuade Jesus to join the Zealots, and Simon is shocked when Jesus asks a tax-collector, Matthew, who works for the hated Romans, to join Him. Meanwhile, Bar-Abbas makes plans to kidnap another tax-collector . . .

MERCY! SPARE MY LIFE, AND I'LL TELL YOU!

VERY WELL!

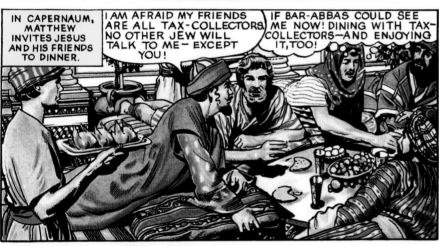

IN CAPERNAUM, MATTHEW INVITES JESUS AND HIS FRIENDS TO DINNER.

I AM AFRAID MY FRIENDS ARE ALL TAX-COLLECTORS. NO OTHER JEW WILL TALK TO ME — EXCEPT YOU!

IF BAR-ABBAS COULD SEE ME NOW! DINING WITH TAX-COLLECTORS — AND ENJOYING IT, TOO!

NOW, SIMON — YOU SAY YOU HAVE A MESSAGE FOR ME?

YES — IT IS THIS...

LATER... SO THAT'S MY ANSWER, SIMON.

VERY WELL, JESUS, I'LL TELL HIM.

SUDDENLY...

LOOK! ELIHU, THE PHARISEE!

HERE, YOU!

WHAT'S YOUR LEADER DOING, EATING WITH THIS DISREPUTABLE LOT?

WHY IS HE MIXING WITH THOSE WHO WORK FOR THE ROMANS?

I DON'T KNOW!

BUT HE WILL — GET HIM, QUICK!

COLLABORATORS!

YOU PHARISEES ARE GOOD AND RESPECTABLE PEOPLE, AREN'T YOU?

WELL—ER—YES.

Bar-Abbas sends Simon to ask Jesus to join the Zealots. Jesus gives Simon His answer at a dinner given by Matthew, a tax-collector. The Pharisees attack Jesus for dining with Matthew: why is He mixing with those who work for the Romans . . . ?

YOU DON'T NEED MY ADVICE AND HELP, DO YOU?

WELL—ER—NO, OF COURSE NOT!

THEN WHY ARE YOU CRITICISING ME BECAUSE I TURN TO THOSE WHO DO?

HOW DID HE MANAGE THAT? I THOUGHT *HE* WAS IN THE WRONG, NOT US!

I'LL HAVE HIM WATCHED NIGHT AND DAY. SOONER OR LATER, WE'RE *BOUND* TO CATCH HIM OUT!

FRANK HAMPSON

SIMON REPORTS BACK TO BAR-ABBAS...

IT'S NO GOOD—JESUS WON'T JOIN US. HE SAYS YOUR WAY IS NOT HIS.

THE FOOL! HE'LL NEVER GET ANYWHERE WITHOUT USING VIOLENCE.

HERE THEY COME!

WHAT'S UP?

TWO OF OUR MEN RETURNING WITH THE RANSOM FOR A TAX-COLLECTOR.

LATER.

A USEFUL SUM. NOW HANG HIM!

NO, NO! YOU PROMISED ME MY LIFE!

BAR-ABBAS! YOUR PROMISE!

A TRICK TO GET HIS MONEY! BESIDES, HE DESERVES TO DIE—HE WORKS FOR THE ROMANS. *STRING HIM UP!*

IF YOU HANG THAT MAN, I GO!

GO! WHERE TO?

TO JOIN JESUS. I PREFER HIS WAY OF TREATING TAX-COLLECTORS!

IT'S GOOD TO HAVE YOU WITH US, SIMON.

THERE ARE THOSE PHARISEES AGAIN.

THEY TAKE IT IN TURNS TO WATCH US.

CAN YOU MAKE OUT WHAT THEY'RE DOING?

Simon the Zealot quarrels with Bar-Abbas over the murder of a tax-collector, and goes off to join Jesus. Meanwhile, the Pharisees – resentful of Jesus's popularity – watch Him in the hope of catching Him doing something wrong as, accompanied by several of His disciples, He walks in the country near Capernaum . .

YES, I CAN.

I'M HUNGRY

DO WHAT I'M DOING. – RUB THE EARS BETWEEN YOUR HANDS AND EAT THE GRAINS.

THEY'RE PICKING THE CORN. THAT COUNTS AS WORK!

AND TODAY'S THE SABBATH...

WE'VE GOT 'EM!

CAUGHT IN THE ACT!

THEY'RE WORKING ON THE SABBATH!

THAT'S AGAINST THE LAW!

WE'RE HUNGRY.

THAT'S NO EXCUSE! GOD WOULD RATHER MEN WENT HUNGRY THAN BROKE HIS LAW.

NONSENSE!

GOD WANTS KINDNESS AND SYMPATHY FROM US, NOT THAT KIND OF SACRIFICE!

THE PHARISEES REPORT BACK...

THEY WERE DEFINITELY BREAKING THE LAW, ELIHU!

DID JESUS DO IT HIMSELF?

NO.

FOOLS! WE'VE GOT TO CATCH *HIM*, NOT HIS FOLLOWERS!

WAIT! I'VE GOT AN IDEA..

SUPPOSE WE SET A TRAP FOR HIM IN THE SYNAGOGUE? LISTEN...

The Pharisees are trying to trap Jesus into breaking the law, which decrees that nobody shall do any work on the sabbath. They lie in wait for Him at the synagogue . . .

HERE HE COMES.

REMEMBER, DON'T SAY A WORD. HE'LL ONLY TWIST IT ROUND AND MAKE US LOOK FOOLS.

LOOK! THAT MAN'S ARM— IT'S A TRAP!

IF JESUS CURES IT TODAY, THEY'LL SAY HE'S BROKEN THE LAW.

AND THEN THERE'LL BE TROUBLE— I HOPE HE DOESN'T.

HE WILL— HE CAN NEVER REFUSE TO HELP SOMEONE.

COME HERE!

WHICH IS WORSE—TO CURE SOMEONE WHO'S ILL, OR TO MAKE PLOTS AND LAY TRAPS?

The Pharisees refuse to reply, and Jesus cures the man of his ailment. Then, a little while later, outside Capernaum . . .

JESUS! THE PHARISEES HAVE COMPLAINED TO HEROD'S MEN.

THEY WANT YOU ARRESTED, LIKE JOHN THE BAPTIST!

I SAID THERE'D BE TROUBLE!

AND JOHN'S DEAD!

THE NEWS HAS JUST COME. HEROD'S HAD HIM EXECUTED!

POOR JOHN— AND NOW I'M IN DANGER.

I MUST NOT BE TAKEN YET...

COLLECT EVERYBODY— WE'LL RETIRE TO THE HILLS TILL THINGS QUIETEN DOWN.

In Jerusalem, High Priest Caiaphas sees a Galilee deputation . . .

HE SAYS HE CAN FORGIVE SINS.

HE CURED SOMEONE ON THE SABBATH.

HE MIXES WITH TAX-COLLECTORS.

PEOPLE ARE WONDERING IF HE'S THE CHRIST.

THAT MUST BE STOPPED, OR THERE'LL BE TROUBLE WITH ROME...

WE MUST TURN THE PEOPLE AGAINST HIM—AND THIS IS HOW TO DO IT...

FRANK HAMPSON

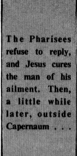

I AM THE SOWER, AND THE SEED IS THE MESSAGE THAT GOD IS OUR FATHER...

Jesus is bitterly attacked by the Pharisees. When He tells a crowd of people the story of the sower, His followers do not understand it, and ask Him what the story means . . .

..IT DOESN'T GET THROUGH TO THE PHARISEES, AND IT DOESN'T LAST WITH THE CROWD, BUT THERE ARE SOME WHO HEAR IT AND CARRY IT OUT IN THEIR LIVES...

NOW SET SAIL!

WHERE TO?

THE OTHER SIDE OF THE LAKE. IT'S NOT HEROD'S TERRITORY, AND WE'LL BE SAFE FROM HIM THERE.

I NEED TIME...

NOT ONE OF YOU IS READY TO CARRY ON IF ANYTHING SHOULD HAPPEN TO ME.

Jesus teaches and trains His disciples, crossing to Galilee at intervals to keep in touch. Finding less opposition than before, He makes a longer stay, remaining in hiding, but sending His disciples out in pairs to teach. Meanwhile, the Zealots in the Galilean hills still want Jesus to join them . . .

HE'S A WONDERFUL SPEAKER.

AND VERY POPULAR— I WISH HE'D JOIN US, BAR-ABBAS.

WELL, HE WON'T— SO WE'VE GOT TO FORCE HIM TO.

HOW?

SUPPOSING WE MIX WITH THE CROWD...

Eventually, the faithful disciples return from teaching . . .

YOU'VE DONE VERY WELL AND DESERVE A REST. WE'LL SAIL DOWN THE LAKE...

... AND FIND A QUIET SPOT, AWAY FROM THE CROWD...

But . . . YOU WANT TO FIND JESUS?

WE KNOW WHERE HE IS. WE'LL LEAD YOU TO HIM!

PEOPLE WILL BEHAVE TO YOU AS YOU BEHAVE TO THEM. THE SECRET OF A HAPPY LIFE IS TO REALIZE THIS AND ACT ON IT.

FRANK HAMPSON

I TOLD YOU HE WAS GOOD, DIDN'T I?

HE CERTAINLY IS! WHEN DO WE START, BAR-ABBAS?

NOT YET, BUT OUR MOMENT WILL COME.

After training His disciples, Jesus sends them out in pairs. On their return, Jesus and the disciples try to get away from the crowd for a rest, but the Zealots have a plan to force Jesus to join their group. They lead the crowd to Jesus, and He teaches them . . .

THEN WE'LL SHARE THAT OUT. . .

GET THEM TO SIT IN GROUPS.

Later . . . THE PEOPLE ARE HUNGRY. HOW MUCH FOOD HAVE WE GOT?

FIVE LOAVES AND A COUPLE OF FISH.

The food is shared out among the groups of hungry people. There is enough food – and more – for everyone. Then Bar-Abbas speaks.

THIS IS IT! GO ROUND, ONE TO A GROUP, AND GET THE CROWD WORKED UP. WHEN I START SHOUTING, TAKE IT UP...

AND THEN HE'LL *HAVE* TO JOIN US—OR BE HAD UP BY ROME FOR TREASON!

MEN! LET'S MAKE JESUS OUR KING!

JESUS! JESUS FOR KING!

KING JESUS! KING JESUS!

JESUS IS OUR CHRIST!

WE MUST STOP THIS! QUICK! GO DOWN TO THE BOAT, ALL OF YOU. I'LL GO THROUGH THE HILLS AND MEET YOU TOMORROW, NEAR CAPERNAUM.

THAT'S NO GOOD. THEY'LL RECOGNIZE YOU AND FOLLOW YOU!

HE INSULTED US PUBLICLY.

AND THEN RAN AWAY WHEN WE CAME TO ARREST HIM.

AT THE MOMENT, THEN, HE IS NO DANGER...

HE'S HIDING SOMEWHERE NOW.

Pharisees from Jerusalem come to arrest Jesus, but He escapes inland — telling His followers He will rejoin them by Lake Galilee. Meanwhile, the Sanhedrin (Jewish Council) meets to hear the Pharisees' report.

BUT WE MUST KEEP HIM UNDER OUR EYE AND WE CAN DO THAT NOW.

HOW?

A MAN IN HIS GANG IS NOT HAPPY ABOUT THE WAY THINGS ARE GOING. HE HAS PROMISED TO KEEP US INFORMED.

WHO IS THIS MAN? WHAT IS HIS NAME?

JUDAS FROM KERIOTH OR, AS SOME CALL HIM, JUDAS ISCARIOT!

Meanwhile, an ambush has been laid in the Galilean hills.

Some weeks later, Jesus returns . . .

WHAT HAVE YOU BEEN DOING?

THINKING OUT WHAT LIES AHEAD OF ME.

OH, AND WHAT'S THAT?

I'LL TELL YOU LATER. FIRST, WE MUST CROSS THE LAKE TO THE PHARISEES AGAIN...

I MUST GIVE THEM ONE MORE CHANCE. THEY MAY HAVE CHANGED THEIR MINDS ABOUT ME.

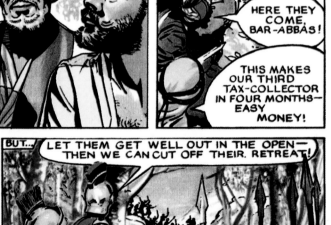

HERE THEY COME, BAR-ABBAS!

THIS MAKES OUR THIRD TAX-COLLECTOR IN FOUR MONTHS— EASY MONEY!

FRANK HAMPSON

CHARGE!

BUT... LET THEM GET WELL OUT IN THE OPEN— THEN WE CAN CUT OFF THEIR RETREAT!

Jesus returns to His followers and takes them across the Lake to Galilee, to see if the Pharisees have changed their minds about Him. In the Galilean hills, Bar-Abbas and his Zealots attack a tax-collector and his Roman escort, not knowing that more Roman soldiers are behind them . . .

Despite the opposition of Herod and Caiaphas, word of Jesus quickly spreads throughout the land of Israel . . .

HE HEALS THE SICK AND MAKES THE BLIND TO SEE.

YOU SHOULD HEAR HIM. I TELL YOU, NO MAN EVER SPOKE LIKE THIS!

YOU SHOULD SEE HIM. HE'S SO STRONG, BUT SO KIND AND GENTLE.

FRANK HAMPSON

HE SAYS WE MUST ALL BE BORN AGAIN...

I BELIEVE HE COMES FROM GOD!

THE HIGH PRIEST CALLS HIM A DEVIL.

HE'S NO DEVIL—HE'S ONE OF THE TRUE OLD PROPHETS OF ISRAEL!

Finding that the Pharisees in Galilee are still hostile, Jesus goes to the area round Caesarea Philippi, north-east of the Lake of Galilee. There, He asks His disciples a question . . .

WHO DO PEOPLE SAY I AM?

JOHN THE BAPTIST, COME BACK TO LIFE.

OR ELIJAH.

BUT YOU, WHO DO YOU SAY I AM?

YOU ARE THE CHRIST.

LISTEN TO ME, ALL OF YOU...

YOU ARE TO TELL NO ONE OF THIS— NO ONE AT ALL!

MUCH SUFFERING LIES AHEAD FOR THE CHRIST, AND DEATH, BUT HE WILL COME BACK TO LIFE AGAIN...

LIFE IS GOING TO BE HARD FOR MY FOLLOWERS IN FUTURE. THEY MUST BE PREPARED TO BE TREATED AS CRIMINALS...

AND NOW WE GO TO JERUSALEM FOR THE PASSOVER.

JERUSALEM? THAT MEANS GOING THROUGH GALILEE...

HOW WILL YOU AVOID HEROD'S MEN?

BY TRAVELLING IN SECRET!

WE'VE GOT TO *DO* SOMETHING! PEOPLE ARE SAYING HE'S THE CHRIST.

IF THAT GOES ON, THERE'LL BE AN UPRISING!

THEN ROME WILL DESTROY JERUSALEM AND WIPE US ALL OUT!

Hearing that Jesus is travelling to Jerusalem for the Passover Festival, Caiaphas – The High Priest – summons a meeting of the Council . . .

WE CANNOT RISK THAT. IT IS BETTER FOR ONE MAN TO DIE, THAN FOR THE WHOLE NATION TO BE DESTROYED...

LET US THEREFORE PLAN HOW WE ARE TO ARREST HIM...

North of the town of Jericho, Jesus joins the Galilean pilgrims who are going to celebrate the Jewish Festival of the Passover. They give him an immensely warm welcome . . .

THAT'S ALL NOW, FRIENDS.

YOU'LL SEE HIM AGAIN IN THE MORNING.

PLEASE CAN WE GO IN? WE'VE BROUGHT OUR CHILDREN TO SEE JESUS.

NO, YOU CAN'T.

HE'S VERY TIRED.

LET THE CHILDREN COME TO ME AND DON'T STOP THEM. THEY HAVE THE SPIRIT OF GOD'S KINGDOM...

THE WAY INTO THE KINGDOM IS THROUGH ACCEPTING GOD AS A LITTLE CHILD DOES.

Then, the following morning . . .

PS'ST, SIMON!

EZRA! WHAT DO YOU WANT? I'VE LEFT THE ZEALOTS.

OH, NO!

I'VE HAD A MESSAGE FROM BAR-ABBAS. HE'S BEEN CAPTURED BY THE ROMANS.

WE'VE COME TO JOIN JESUS. WE WANT HIM TO LEAD US IN AN ATTACK ON THE ROMAN GARRISON!

FRANK HAMPSON

ARMED MEN ARE HIDING IN BETHANY...

Hearing that Jesus is coming to Jerusalem for the Passover Festival, Caiaphas – the High Priest – orders His arrest. At Jericho, a messenger from the Zealots (the underground movement against Rome) tells Simon that they want Jesus to lead them in an attack on the Roman garrison at Jerusalem.

AND, AMONG THE DONKEYS FOR HIRE, IS A WAR-HORSE FOR JESUS. THE PASSWORD IS: 'THE LEADER NEEDS HIM'.

THE TIME HAS COME TO STRIKE! ALL THE ZEALOT BANDS ARE CONVERGING SECRETLY ON JERUSALEM.

WITH JESUS AT OUR HEAD, WE WILL STORM THE GATES, SEIZE THE CITY, AND PROCLAIM JESUS KING OF THE JEWS.

SUPPOSING JESUS COMES IN PEACE, NOT WAR?

THEN LET HIM TAKE ONE OF THE DONKEYS INSTEAD.

Pondering the desperate plan of his former comrades, Simon leaves the Zealots and rejoins Jesus, who is talking to His disciples . . .

THE WAY TO BE IMPORTANT IN MY KINGDOM IS NOT TO LORD IT OVER THE REST...

BUT TO PUT YOURSELF OUT TO SERVE THEM, JUST AS I HAVE COME TO SERVE OTHERS...

AND TO GIVE MY LIFE FOR THEM.

Some time later, beside one of the gates of Jerusalem . . .

MEN, THE COUNCIL HAS ORDERED US TO ARREST THIS FELLOW JESUS, BUT QUIETLY, SO AS TO AVOID A RIOT.

SERGEANT!

JESUS IS TWO MILES OFF—HE'S JUST ENTERING BETHANY!

FRANK HAMPSON.

Jesus enters the city of Jerusalem in triumph. He goes straight to the Temple, and turns out the traders who have set up their stalls there . . .

OUTSIDE, ALL OF YOU! THIS PLACE IS MEANT FOR PRAYER, NOT ROBBING AND CHEATING!

FRANK HAMPSON

Angry priests come up . . . HERE, YOU! WHAT DO YOU THINK YOU'RE DOING?

WHO GAVE YOU PERMISSION TO TAKE MATTERS INTO YOUR OWN HANDS LIKE THIS?

I'LL ANSWER THAT, IF YOU'LL ANSWER THIS — WAS JOHN THE BAPTIST INSPIRED BY GOD...

...OR WAS HE A FAKE?

WHAT DO WE SAY? FROM GOD?

BUT THEN HE'LL SAY, "WHY DIDN'T YOU LISTEN TO HIM?"

THEN WE'LL SAY HE WAS A FAKE.

HERE, DON'T YOU SAY THAT! JOHN WAS A PROPHET!

WE-ER—DON'T KNOW.

THAT'S A PITY BECAUSE, IF YOU DID...

...YOU'D KNOW WHY I ACT AS I DO!

Later . . . THE MAN'S UTTERLY IMPOSSIBLE!

YOU CAN'T PIN HIM DOWN!

NONSENSE — I CAN! WHERE IS HE NOW?

HE'S TALKING TO A CROWD IN THE UNFINISHED PART OF THE TEMPLE, WHERE THE WORKMEN ARE.

GOOD! I'LL SHOW HIM UP IN FRONT OF *THEM*, AND EVERYBODY ELSE...

COME ON—THEY'LL SOON BE USING THEIR STONES TO THROW AT HIM!

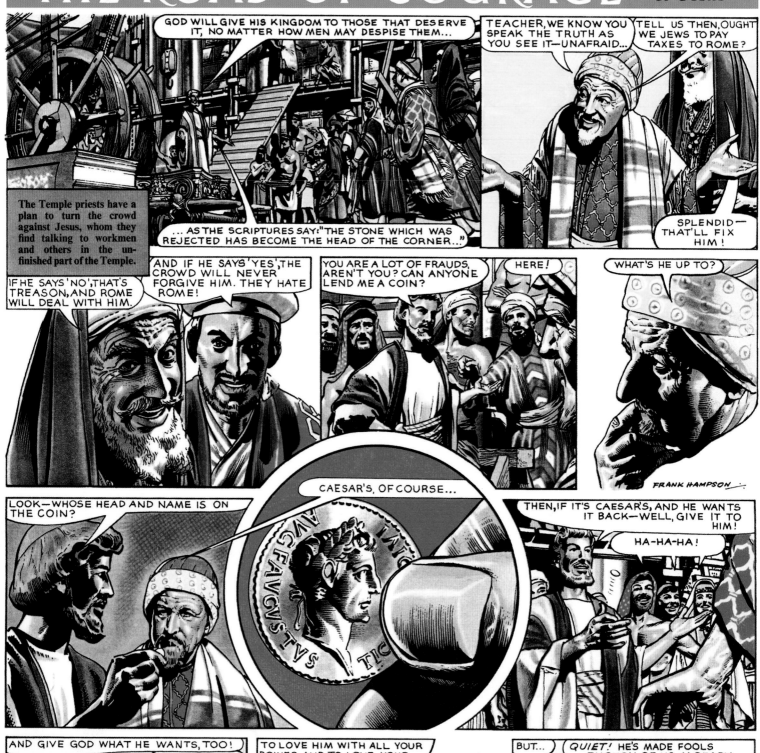

GOD WILL GIVE HIS KINGDOM TO THOSE THAT DESERVE IT, NO MATTER HOW MEN MAY DESPISE THEM...

TEACHER, WE KNOW YOU SPEAK THE TRUTH AS YOU SEE IT—UNAFRAID...

TELL US THEN, OUGHT WE JEWS TO PAY TAXES TO ROME?

The Temple priests have a plan to turn the crowd against Jesus, whom they find talking to workmen and others in the unfinished part of the Temple.

... AS THE SCRIPTURES SAY: "THE STONE WHICH WAS REJECTED HAS BECOME THE HEAD OF THE CORNER..."

SPLENDID— THAT'LL FIX HIM!

AND IF HE SAYS 'YES', THE CROWD WILL NEVER FORGIVE HIM. THEY HATE ROME!

IF HE SAYS 'NO', THAT'S TREASON, AND ROME WILL DEAL WITH HIM.

YOU ARE A LOT OF FRAUDS, AREN'T YOU? CAN ANYONE LEND ME A COIN?

HERE!

WHAT'S HE UP TO?

FRANK HAMPSON

CAESAR'S, OF COURSE...

LOOK—WHOSE HEAD AND NAME IS ON THE COIN?

THEN, IF IT'S CAESAR'S, AND HE WANTS IT BACK—WELL, GIVE IT TO HIM!

HA-HA-HA!

AND GIVE GOD WHAT HE WANTS, TOO!

AND WHAT MAY THAT BE?

TO LOVE HIM WITH ALL YOUR POWER, AND TO LOVE YOUR FELLOW MEN AS YOU DO YOURSELVES. ALL TRUE RELIGION DEPENDS ON OUR DOING THESE TWO THINGS.

BUT...

QUIET! HE'S MADE FOOLS ENOUGH OF US ALREADY.

NOT FOR LONG. CAIAPHAS MUST STRIKE NOW!

For three days, Jesus speaks to large and enthusiastic crowds in the Temple courts at Jerusalem. To His disciples, everything is going well; then, on the Wednesday morning . . .

TWO DAYS TO THE PASSOVER, WHEN THE CHRIST IS GOING TO BE BETRAYED AND PUT TO DEATH...

HOW CAN HE TALK LIKE THAT, JAMES?

I DON'T UNDERSTAND IT, ANDREW. THE WHOLE CITY'S ON HIS SIDE!

HE CAN MAKE HIMSELF KING ANY TIME NOW!

I WONDER WHEN HE WILL?

But the priests are not on Jesus's side. In the Temple, Caiaphas listens to his sly old father-in-law, Annas, himself a former High Priest . . .

TWO DAYS TO THE PASSOVER, AND HE'S STILL FREE...

HE'S ALWAYS IN THE MIDDLE OF CROWDS. IF ONLY WE COULD CATCH HIM ALONE.

WE CAN!

JUDAS ISCARIOT HAS PROMISED TO TELL US WHERE WE CAN ARREST HIM QUIETLY AT NIGHT.

GOOD, GOOD! WE MUST REWARD JUDAS.

THAT HAS BEEN ARRANGED. HE'LL GET THIRTY PIECES OF SILVER.

In an upstairs room in Jerusalem, on Thursday evening . . .

THIS IS MY LAST SUPPER WITH YOU.

WHAT DO YOU MEAN?

ONE OF YOU IS GOING TO BETRAY ME...

BETRAY YOU? ONE OF US?

FRANK HAMPSON

The Last Supper is over, and Jesus sets out for Gethsemane with His followers – except for Judas, who has gone to the house of Caiaphas, the High Priest, with the information that Jesus can at last be arrested without a disturbance being caused . . .

GO WITH THE GUARD, JUDAS, AND SHOW THEM WHICH IS JESUS.

WELL DONE, JUDAS, YOU'RE DOING A GOOD JOB!

GUARD DETAIL — MARCH!

AM I? OR AM I BETRAYING AN INNOCENT MAN?

WE MUST SUMMON THE COUNCIL AND TRY HIM IMMEDIATELY — FINISH IT ALL OFF BEFORE THE SABBATH CAN DELAY IT.

I AGREE. DELAY IS DANGEROUS — HIS GANG COULD STIR UP THE PEOPLE TO RESCUE HIM.

A little earlier, the disciples – feeling anxious and a little uneasy – approached Gethsemane with Jesus . . .

IS THAT A SWORD, PETER?

YES, I BORROWED IT YESTERDAY — JUST IN CASE.

YOU WILL ALL LOSE YOUR FAITH IN ME TONIGHT.

LOSE OUR FAITH IN YOU? THE OTHERS MAY, BUT I WON'T!

PETER, BEFORE THE SECOND COCK-CROW, YOU WILL THREE TIMES DENY YOU'VE EVER KNOWN ME.

I WON'T — I'LL DIE BEFORE I DO THAT!

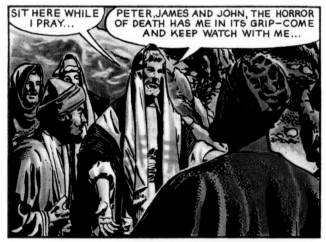

SIT HERE WHILE I PRAY . . .

PETER, JAMES AND JOHN, THE HORROR OF DEATH HAS ME IN ITS GRIP — COME AND KEEP WATCH WITH ME . . .

FATHER, IF IT BE POSSIBLE, DO NOT LET ME HAVE TO GO THROUGH WITH THIS . . .

YET, IF I MUST, LET ME CARRY OUT YOUR WISHES.

FRANK HAMPSON

While Jesus is praying, three disciples fall fast asleep. Then, some time later . . .

ASLEEP, PETER? WAKE UP! MY BETRAYER IS COMING . . .

EH? WHAT'S THAT?

MASTER!

ARREST THAT MAN!

JUDAS, YOU TRAITOR!

TO THE RESCUE MEN!

TAKE THAT!

STOP FIGHTING!

DO YOU THINK I COULDN'T RAISE AN ARMY IF I WISHED? BUT THOSE WHO TAKE THE SWORD, DIE BY THE SWORD...

When Jesus is arrested at Gethsemane by Roman soldiers, His loyal followers fight to rescue Him...

BESIDES, THE SCRIPTURES SAY IT MUST HAPPEN LIKE THIS...

LET THE OTHERS GO, CAPTAIN. I'M THE MAN YOU WANT!

The disciples break, and run off into the night...

EVERYONE ELSE MAY RUN AWAY, BUT I WON'T...

THEY'RE TAKING HIM INTO THE HIGH PRIEST'S HOUSE...

I'LL RISK IT AND SLIP IN AFTER THEM.

THAT MAN WAS WITH JESUS!

YOU'RE WRONG, MY GIRL—I DON'T KNOW HIM!

YOU *ARE* ONE OF THEM, YOU KNOW.

MAN, I'M *NOT!*

Elsewhere in the house, the trial begins; but it does not run smoothly and, an hour later, the High Priest rises to his feet...

FRANK HAMPSON

GENTLEMEN, THIS IS HOPELESS — THE WITNESSES ARE CONTRADICTING EACH OTHER. I WILL THEREFORE EXAMINE THE PRISONER MYSELF.

IS THAT LEGAL?

BARELY, BUT WE *MUST* DO IT. WE CAN'T LET HIM GO NOW.

PRISONER, YOU HAVE HEARD THE EVIDENCE AGAINST YOU. IS IT TRUE?

SILENT, EH? THEN I COMMAND YOU, AS YOU BELIEVE IN GOD, TO ANSWER ME...

ARE YOU CHRIST, THE SON OF GOD?

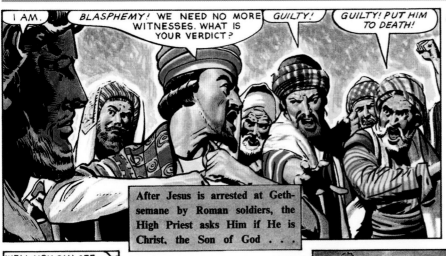

I AM.

BLASPHEMY! WE NEED NO MORE WITNESSES. WHAT IS YOUR VERDICT?

GUILTY!

GUILTY! PUT HIM TO DEATH!

After Jesus is arrested at Gethsemane by Roman soldiers, the High Priest asks Him if He is Christ, the Son of God . . .

In the Courtyard outside the High Priest's house, Peter is at bay . . .

YOU *ARE* ONE OF THEM!

YOU'RE A GALILEAN, LIKE HIM.

YOUR ACCENT GIVES YOU AWAY.

I SWEAR BY HEAVEN THAT I DON'T KNOW THE MAN!

WELL, YOU CAN SEE HIM NOW. THEY'RE BRINGING HIM OUT.

ABOUT TIME, TOO. IT'S SECOND COCK-CROW.

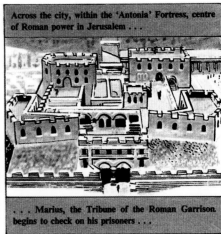

Across the city, within the 'Antonia' Fortress, centre of Roman power in Jerusalem . . .

. . . Marius, the Tribune of the Roman Garrison, begins to check on his prisoners . . .

THIS IS BAR-ABBAS, THE REBEL. HE'S DUE FOR EXECUTION THIS AFTERNOON.

SIR . . .

HIS EXCELLENCY, THE GOVERNOR, WANTS YOU.

YOU SENT FOR ME, PONTIUS PILATE?

YES, MARIUS. THE PRIESTS WANT ME TO EXECUTE A MAN CALLED JESUS OF NAZARETH. HOW MUCH DO WE KNOW ABOUT HIM?

FRANK HAMPSON

HE'S GOT A FOLLOWING OF SORTS—PEASANTS, MOSTLY.

DANGEROUS?

DOESN'T SEEM TO BE.

H'M — THE PRIESTS ACCUSE HIM OF BLASPHEMY . . .

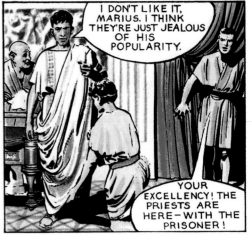

I DON'T LIKE IT, MARIUS. I THINK THEY'RE JUST JEALOUS OF HIS POPULARITY.

YOUR EXCELLENCY! THE PRIESTS ARE HERE—WITH THE PRISONER!

THE PRIESTS ARE AT THE GATE, SIRE. THE LAWS OF THEIR RELIGION FORBID THEM TO ENTER, FOR FEAR OF DEFILEMENT.

I WILL GO OUT.

Jesus's death-sentence for blasphemy is confirmed by the Sanhedrin – Jewish Council – but He cannot be executed without the consent of Pontius Pilate, the Roman Governor. Blasphemy is not punishable by death under Roman Law, so Caiaphas accuses Jesus of treason, taking him to Pilate in the 'Antonia' Fortress.

FRANK HAMPSON

WHAT ARE YOUR CHARGES, HIGH PRIEST?

TREASON! HE INCITES REVOLT AND CLAIMS HE'S A KING.

Deeply perturbed, Pontius Pilate takes Jesus into his palace and puts some questions to Him . . .

ARE YOU KING OF THE JEWS?

YES, BUT MY REALM DOES NOT BELONG TO *THIS* WORLD...

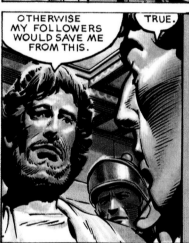

OTHERWISE MY FOLLOWERS WOULD SAVE ME FROM THIS.

TRUE.

Later, realizing that Jesus is a Galilean, Pilate sends Him to Herod Antipas, ruler of Galilee, who is in the City. But Antipas merely mocks Him, arrays Him in 'gorgeous apparel', and returns Him to Pontius Pilate . . .

I CAN FIND NOTHING WRONG ABOUT HIM. I SHALL WHIP HIM AND RELEASE HIM.

CRUCIFY HIM! CRUCIFY HIM!

THEY'RE LOOKING UGLY, MARIUS...

I DAREN'T RISK A RIOT. I HAVE STRICT ORDERS FROM ROME TO KEEP THE PEACE...

WAIT, THOUGH. IT IS THE CUSTOM THAT THE JEWS CHOOSE A PRISONER TO BE SET FREE AT PASSOVER TIME.

JESUS!

WE WANT JESUS!

YES—THAT'S WHAT MOST OF THE CROWD HAVE COME FOR...

THOSE AT THE BACK ARE STARTING TO SHOUT – FOR JESUS!

WE WANT JESUS—*BAR-ABBAS!*

SET FREE JESUS!

YES! SET FREE JESUS – *JESUS BAR-ABBAS!*

SET FREE JESUS BAR-ABBAS!

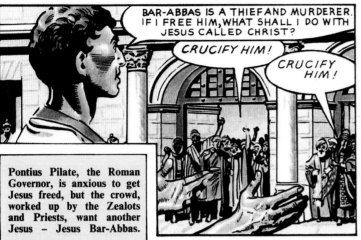

BAR-ABBAS IS A THIEF AND MURDERER. IF I FREE HIM, WHAT SHALL I DO WITH JESUS CALLED CHRIST?

CRUCIFY HIM!

CRUCIFY HIM!

Pontius Pilate, the Roman Governor, is anxious to get Jesus freed, but the crowd, worked up by the Zealots and Priests, want another Jesus – Jesus Bar-Abbas.

Hoping to placate the Priests and wring mercy from the crowd, Pilate has Jesus scourged. The soldiers give him a mock 'crown' of thorns and a 'royal' robe. Then Pilate brings him before the people again . . .

BEHOLD THE MAN!

SHALL I CRUCIFY YOUR KING?

WE HAVE NO KING BUT CAESAR!

YOU'RE NO FRIEND OF CAESAR'S IF YOU REPRIEVE HIM!

THEY'VE GOT ME, MARIUS. I DAREN'T RISK A COMPLAINT TO ROME.

BRING ME THE WARRANT—AND SOME WATER...

I AM INNOCENT OF THE BLOOD OF THIS JUST MAN. THE RESPONSIBILITY IS YOURS...

TAKE HIM AND CRUCIFY HIM!

HE GAVE THEM THE CHOICE, AND THEY CHOSE BAR-ABBAS —BAR-ABBAS!

THEY'RE COMING!

Later, in an upper room, Simon reports to the disciples, who wait with Mary, Mother of Jesus, and Mary Magdalene . . .

THERE'S NO HOPE, THEN.

FRANK HAMPSON

On Calvary, the execution hill just outside Jerusalem, Jesus is prepared for crucifixion with two criminals . . .

FATHER, FORGIVE THEM, FOR THEY KNOW NOT WHAT THEY DO.

As the soldiers gambled for His clothing, in a darkness like an impending storm, Jesus endured the slow agony of the Cross. The Priests of the Temple came out to jeer at their victim, and the people of Jerusalem laughed and mocked at His sufferings, and Jesus gave a great cry: "My God, My God, why hast thou forsaken me?"

HE SAVED OTHERS, BUT HE CAN'T SAVE HIMSELF.

I'LL BELIEVE HE'S THE CHRIST WHEN I SEE HIM COME DOWN FROM THE CROSS!

HO-HO! SO WILL I.

HI, YOU! WHY DON'T YOU SAVE YOURSELF?

COME ON, STEP DOWN!

BE QUIET!

I KNOW HE REFUSED TO TAKE THE WAR-HORSE, BUT PILATE WANTED *ME* UP THERE. HE'S DYING INSTEAD OF ME.

YOU'RE RIGHT THERE. HE'S DYING INSTEAD OF VERY MANY WORSE MEN . . .

TRULY HE MUST BE THE SON OF GOD!

FRANK HAMPSON

After the crucifixion, the body of Jesus is hastily placed in a tomb belonging to Joseph of Arimathea. At dawn on the Sunday, Mary Magdalene and other women go to the tomb to anoint the body, in accordance with the custom . . .

MARY MAGDALENE, THERE'S A STONE IN FRONT OF THE TOMB. WHO'S GOING TO MOVE IT FOR US?

LOOK! THE STONE HAS BEEN ROLLED BACK!

DON'T BE FRIGHTENED. ARE YOU LOOKING FOR JESUS WHO WAS CRUCIFIED? HE IS NOT HERE . . .

HE HAS RISEN! GO AND TELL HIS FOLLOWERS, AND PETER.

But the women are frightened, and run away.

PETER! JOHN! COME QUICKLY — SOMETHING HORRIBLE'S HAPPENED!

WHAT IS IT?

THE BODY'S GONE! THEY'VE TAKEN IT AWAY. WE DON'T KNOW WHERE THEY'VE PUT IT!

FRANK HAMPSON

Peter and John go to the tomb and find it empty. Puzzled, they return to the house. Mary Magdalene remains alone by the tomb, weeping . . .

MARY!

MASTER!

MY GIRL, WHY ARE YOU CRYING? WHO ARE YOU LOOKING FOR?

OH, SIR, ARE YOU THE GARDENER HERE? IF YOU HAVE REMOVED THE BODY, PLEASE TELL ME WHERE YOU HAVE PUT HIM, AND I WILL TAKE HIM AWAY.

On the Sunday evening, Jesus's followers excitedly discuss Mary's astonishing news . . .

MARY MAGDALENE SWEARS SHE SAW HIM AND HE SPOKE TO HER... AND CLEOPAS IS CONVINCED THEY MET HIM GOING TO EMMAUS.... IF ONLY WE COULD BELIEVE IT.

PEACE BE TO YOU ALL! IT'S HIS GHOST!

DON'T BE AFRAID— IT REALLY IS ME! GHOSTS DON'T HAVE FLESH AND BLOOD, BUT YOU CAN SEE I HAVE.

HAVE YOU ANYTHING TO EAT? THERE'S SOME FISH. AND A PIECE OF HONEYCOMB.

DON'T YOU REMEMBER HOW I TOLD YOU THE SCRIPTURES SAID ALL THIS WOULD HAPPEN? THAT THE CHRIST WOULD BE PUT TO DEATH AND THEN COME BACK FROM THE DEAD?

AND NOW ALL MANKIND MUST BE TOLD OF WHAT HE HAS DONE... ...AND BE URGED TO CHANGE THEIR WHOLE OUTLOOK... ...WIPE OUT ALL THEIR PAST LIFE AND MAKE A FRESH START.

YOU HAVE BEEN EYE-WITNESSES OF ALL THIS, AND SO I NOW HAND OVER TO YOU THE MESSAGE OF THE FATHER...

SPREAD THE GOOD NEWS TO ALL THE WORLD. TEACH THEM WHAT I HAVE TAUGHT YOU — AND REMEMBER...

FRANK HAMPSON.

I AM WITH YOU ALWAYS - EVEN TO THE END OF THE WORLD.

THE END

MARK

THE YOUNGEST
DISCIPLE

WRITTEN BY
CHAD VARAH

DRAWN BY
GIORGIO BELLAVITIS

MARK THE YOUNGEST DISCIPLE

The life story of JOHN MARK writer of the 2nd Gospel

Jerusalem, March, A.D.29. It is just before the Festival called "Passover", and the city is full of pilgrims. The Roman Governor has brought in extra troops to keep order. Everyone is excited about the young prophet from Galilee, Jesus of Nazareth, wondering if he can be the "Christ" (the King sent by God) promised in the Jewish Scriptures. The Chief Priests are jealous of his popularity and are plotting to kill him; but he is surrounded by crowds during the day, and at night he leaves the city. They don't know what house he will go to for the Festival . . .

STORY BY CHAD VARAH: DRAWN BY BELLAVITIS.

MOTHER, WHEN ARE WE GOING TO SEE JESUS AGAIN? HE DIDN'T COME TO THE CITY YESTERDAY.

I CAN'T TELL YOU, MARK.

Mark's home, Thursday.

YOU RANG, MADAM?

YES. I HAVE AN IMPORTANT ERRAND FOR YOU. I WANT YOU TO TAKE A WATER-PITCHER . . .

A WATER-PITCHER? BUT THAT'S WOMAN'S WORK, MADAM!

PRECISELY. IT WILL SINGLE YOU OUT FROM OTHER SERVANTS.

VERY WELL, MADAM.

RUN ALONG NOW, DEAR. THIS IS NOTHING TO DO WITH LITTLE BOYS.

GO TO THE FOUNTAIN BY THE FISH GATE . . .

"LITTLE BOYS", INDEED! I WONDER IF IT'S SOMETHING TO DO WITH JESUS? FISH GATE, HUH?

HEY! WHY DON'T YOU LOOK WHERE YOU'RE GOING?

SORRY, SIR—URGENT BUSINESS!

THAT MAN MUST BE A MAID-OF-ALL-WORK!

HA! HA!

I'LL TRY THE PASSWORD, JOHN.

THAT'LL BE THE CHAP, PETER.

THE MASTER SAYS, WHERE'S THE ROOM WHERE I'M TO HAVE SUPPER WITH MY DISCIPLES?

FOLLOW ME—AT A DISTANCE.

PETER! JOHN!

WHAT ARE YOU DOING HERE, YOUNG MARCUS?

HOPING TO GET NEWS OF JESUS. IS HE COMING TO OUR HOUSE TO-NIGHT?

QUIET, BOY! DO YOU REALIZE IT MIGHT HAVE COST HIM HIS LIFE IF A SPY HAD HEARD YOU?

CONTINUED

The life story of
JOHN MARK
writer of the 2nd Gospel

Jerusalem, March, A.D.29. Pilgrims from all over the world are excited about the young prophet from Galilee, Jesus of Nazareth, wondering if he is the "Christ", the Divine King promised in the Jewish Scriptures. The authorities are jealous of his popularity and would arrest him if they could catch him away from the crowds. One Thursday, Mark follows a servant sent out mysteriously by his mother, and finds him bringing back Peter and John, two of Jesus's disciples, to prepare supper for "the Master". Mark asks if Jesus is coming that night - and Peter tells the boy it might have cost Jesus his life if a spy had overheard!

STORY BY CHAD VARAH: DRAWN BY BELLAVITIS.

I—I'M S-SORRY, PETER! I—I NEVER REALIZED THAT "YOU-KNOW-WHO" WAS IN DANGER!

WELL, HE IS.

B-BUT EVERYBODY LOVES HIM...

NOT EVERYBODY, MARK. BUT *YOU* DO — SO RUN ALONG BEFORE WE ATTRACT ANY MORE ATTENTION

I CAN'T BELIEVE IT! HE HEALS THE SICK, HELPS THE POOR, MAKES GOD REAL TO US — WHO COULD HATE HIM FOR *THAT*?

HEY, LAD! HELP ME TO SET THIS DOWN A MINUTE.

STEADY!

I'VE GOT IT — PHEW!

THANKS, BOY. NEEDED A REST.

I'LL LOAD YOU UP AGAIN WHEN YOU'RE READY — I SAY, TELL ME...

...WHAT DO YOU THINK OF JESUS?

'E SUITS *ME*. I COULD LISTEN TO 'IM FOR HOURS. BUT 'E'S TOO GOOD FOR THIS WORLD. THEY'LL GET 'IM — YOU MARK MY WORDS!

"GET HIM"? WHO?

WHY, THE HIGH PRIEST AND HIS PALS. THEY'D SOON LOSE THEIR JOBS IF JESUS TOOK OVER. IT'S 'IM OR THEM — MORE'S THE PITY!

MIND YOU, THEY'D 'AVE TO CATCH 'IM ON 'IS OWN. SHOVE HARDER, LAD! 'E WANTS TO KEEP AWAY FROM THE CITY TONIGHT.

BIG DAY TOMORROW. IF JESUS WAS PROCLAIMED KING, THEY'D 'AVE HAD IT. THANKS FOR HELPING!

WHY TONIGHT?

TONIGHT! AND JESUS *IS* COMING! I MUST WARN HIM...

CONTINUED

The life story of
JOHN MARK,
writer of the 2nd Gospel

March, A.D.29. Jerusalem is in a ferment over Jesus, the young prophet from Nazareth. His fellow-Galileans and other pilgrims believe he is the promised "Christ", but the Chief Priests fear his popularity and want to kill him. During the day he is protected by the common people, and at night he leaves the city, so they can't catch him alone. One Thursday he sends Peter and John, two of his twelve disciples, to prepare a secret supper at Mark's mother's house. Mark is delighted — until he hears a labourer say the authorities will stake everything on arresting Jesus that night, lest the people should proclaim him King at the Festival next day. Mark decides he must warn Jesus to keep away from the city...

STORY BY CHAD VARAH:
DRAWN BY BELLAVITIS.

BUY MY FRESH HONEY-CAKES!

ALMS, FOR THE LOVE OF GOD!

EXCUSE ME, PLEASE!

BEST BETHANY OIL! OLIVE OIL!

GIDDAP!

JESUS HAS BEEN STAYING AT BETHANY — I MUST GET THERE BEFORE HE LEAVES...

After crossing over the brook called Kedron, Mark has a couple of miles to run...

... and eventually arrives at Bethany almost exhausted.

I WONDER IF THIS IS LAZARUS' HOUSE? IF I COULD SEE SOMEONE I KNEW...

SPYING, EH? AND WHO MIGHT YOU BE LOOKING FOR, YOUNG FELLER-ME-LAD?

A—A FRIEND, LEMME GO!

NOT TILL WE FIND OUT WHO SENT YOU. P'RAPS THEY THOUGHT A LAD WOULDN'T BE NOTICED!

NO ONE SENT ME! I CAME TO SEE IF JESUS WAS STILL HERE...

HA! JUST AS I THOUGHT! WELL, I'M NOT TELLING YOU — AND YOU SHALL STAY WHERE YOU WON'T FIND OUT!

LET ME OUT! HE'S IN DANGER — I CAME TO WARN HIM...

WHY, IT'S JOHN MARK — MARY'S SON, FROM JERUSALEM! YOU POOR BOY!

HOW WAS I TO KNOW? THERE'VE BEEN THREE SPIES TODAY ALREADY, LAZARUS!

Some hours later...

YOU MUST REST WHILE WE GET YOU SOME FOOD.

NO THANK YOU, LAZARUS — I MUST GET HOME AS QUICK AS I CAN.

I'LL BE TOO LATE TO STOP HIM COMING, BUT I CAN KEEP WATCH...

CONTINUED

The life story of
JOHN MARK
writer of the 2nd Gospel

A Thursday in March, A.D.29. Mark has discovered that the Jewish authorities are planning to arrest Jesus if they can find him in Jerusalem at night without the crowds, who believe he is the Christ, to protect him. And Mark knows that his own mother's house is being prepared for Jesus to have supper with his twelve disciples that very night! He runs all the way to the village of Bethany, where Jesus has been staying, to warn him not to enter the city, but while he is looking over the wall of Lazarus's house, a burly Galilean takes him for a spy and locks him up in the house. By the time Lazarus comes back and recognizes him and lets him out, it is too late to do anything but go home and stand guard.

STORY BY CHAD VARAH:
DRAWN BY BELLAVITIS.

WHY DID HE GO TO THE CITY? HE WAS SAFE WITH ALL THESE GALILEANS CAMPING ROUND HIM... NO SIGN OF THE TEMPLE GUARD...

MARK! WHEREVER HAVE YOU BEEN?

AT LAZARUS'S HOUSE, MOTHER. I'M SORRY I MADE YOU ANXIOUS.

I MISSED JESUS AT BETHANY. HAS — HAS HE ARRIVED?

YES, SOME TIME AGO. NOW, OFF TO BED WITH YOU! YOU CAN SLEEP ON THE ROOF IF YOU LIKE.

I *DO* WANT TO SEE JESUS! I KNOW — LET ME GO AND BATHE THE VISITORS' FEET!

JESUS DID THAT HUMBLE TASK HIMSELF.

HIMSELF? OUR LORD DID A SERVANT'S JOB...?

TALKING OF WASHING, JUST LOOK AT YOU! GO AND GET YOURSELF CLEAN, MY LAD, AND THEN *STRAIGHT* OFF TO BED!

GOD BLESS YOU, DEAR. DON'T FORGET YOUR PRAYERS.

I NEVER DO, MOTHER. GOOD NIGHT!

I'LL GET THE BOWL AND TOWEL FROM THE UPPER ROOM — THAT'LL GIVE ME AN EXCUSE TO SEE JESUS...

HA, THERE IT IS, JUST INSIDE THE DOOR...

THIS IS MY BODY...

THAT'S JESUS'S VOICE — WHAT *CAN* HE MEAN?

HE MUST MEAN HE'S GOING TO BE KILLED!

IF HE KNOWS, WHAT'S THE GOOD OF WARNING HIM? BUT I WON'T LET HIM BE KILLED! I WON'T, I WON'T!

CONTINUED

The life story of JOHN MARK, writer of the 2nd Gospel

A Thursday night in March, A.D.29. Mark hasn't been able to find Jesus in time to warn him *not* to come into Jerusalem that night, as the authorities will arrest him if they can catch him away from the Jewish crowds who love him. But Jesus and his twelve special friends are safe as long as the Priests don't know they're having supper in the upstairs room at Mark's home. On his way up to bed on the flat roof, Mark quietly opens the door of the upper room to get the washing bowl used by the visitors, and sees Jesus break a flat bread-cake, saying "This is my body". Jesus must mean that he *knows* he's going to be killed — so what's the good of warning him? Nevertheless, Mark determines to do all he possibly can to protect him.

STORY BY CHAD VARAH: DRAWN BY BELLAVITIS.

P'RAPS JESUS DIDN'T MEAN HE WOULD BE KILLED. HIS ENEMIES THINK HE'S SAFE AT BETHANY...

NONE OF US WOULD THINK OF GIVING HIM AWAY, AND THE PRIESTS HAVE NO REASON TO SUSPECT HE'S HERE...

ALL THE SAME, I'LL STAY AWAKE AND KEEP GUARD...

BETTER GET UNDRESSED, THOUGH, IN CASE MOTHER COMES UP TO SEE IF I'M IN BED...

THERE. IF MUM COMES, I CAN HOP INTO BED, AND IF IT'S ANYONE ELSE...

ALL WELL SO FAR — BUT I MUSTN'T FALL ASLEEP.

But soon Mark falls into an uneasy doze.

WH-WHAT WAS THAT? A DOOR SLAMMED.

IT WAS I, JUDAS, JESUS LOOKED AT WHEN HE SAID "ONE OF YOU SHALL BETRAY ME"...

IT'S NOT "BETRAYING" HIM TO FORCE HIM TO PROVE HIS POWER. IF HE'S THE CHRIST, GOD WILL PROTECT HIM — AND IF NOT...

WHAT ON EARTH DID JUDAS MEAN? IT SOUNDED ALMOST AS IF... BUT NO, HE *COULDN'T*...

IF I FOLLOW HIM, THERE'LL BE NO ONE TO KEEP WATCH HERE — OH, WHAT *CAN* I DO TO SAVE JESUS?

CONTINUED

The life story of
JOHN MARK,
writer of the 2nd Gospel

A Thursday night in March, A.D.29. Mark knows that the Chief Priests want to arrest Jesus that very night, if they can catch him in Jerusalem unprotected by the crowds who believe he is the Christ — and Jesus has come with his twelve chief followers to have supper in Mark's mother's big upstairs room! Mark is sent to bed on the roof, but decides to stay awake and keep watch. Eventually he dozes, and wakes when Judas, one of the disciples, leaves the upper room and slams the door. Mark hears Judas muttering something about 'betraying', and doesn't know whether to follow Judas or stay on guard. What can he do to save Jesus?

STORY BY CHAD VARAH: DRAWN BY BELLAVITIS.

HE LOOKS FURTIVE. THAT SETTLES IT — I'LL FOLLOW HIM . . .

IF JESUS *REALLY* SAID ONE OF THEM WAS A TRAITOR, HE WON'T STAY HERE MUCH LONGER . . .

I'M TRACKING HIM QUITE WELL — HE HASN'T REALIZED ANYONE'S FOLLOWING HIM . . .

HE'S STOPPED — I'LL TRY TO GET CLOSER. IF HE'S GOING TO THE HIGH PRIEST, HE'LL TURN LEFT . . .

IT'S JESUS'S OWN FAULT — HE SHOULD HAVE BEEN GUIDED BY ME, JUDAS. I'M THE ONLY CLEVER ONE AMONG THEM . . .

IT'S NOT THE MONEY THEY OFFERED — WHAT'S THIRTY PIECES OF SILVER? THE PRICE OF A SLAVE! STILL, I'LL NOT REFUSE IT . . .

OH GOD! JUDAS! STOP!

NOT SO FAST! YOU CAN'T GO IN THERE!

MUST SEE — HIGH PRIEST — URGENT — OUT OF MY WAY!

OH, IT'S YOU AT LAST, JUDAS ISCARIOT! IN YOU GO — HIS HOLINESS IS WAITING FOR YOU!

PLEASE, PLEASE, I *MUST* SPEAK TO JUDAS ISCARIOT — I MUST!

WHAT DO YOU WANT, BOY? 'OP IT OR YOU'LL FIND YOURSELF IN A CELL, WITH A THICK EAR.

CONTINUED

The life story of
JOHN MARK,
writer of the 2nd Gospel

A Thursday night in March, A.D.29. While Jesus and his followers are having supper in a room at Mark's home, Mark has been keeping watch on the roof, where he sleeps in spring and summer, because he knows the High Priests want to arrest Jesus if they can catch him unprotected. Mark sees Judas, one of the disciples, leave furtively, muttering something about "betrayal", and decides to follow him. He trails him unperceived and hears enough to confirm his suspicions; but Judas suddenly darts into the High Priests' courtyard, and the guard won't let Mark follow. In fact, he threatens to lock him up unless he clears off.

STORY BY CHAD VARAH:
DRAWN BY BELLAVITIS.

IF ONLY I KNEW WHAT WAS GOING ON IN THERE — IT'S TERRIBLE TO SUSPECT THAT JUDAS IS...

A TRAITOR! THAT'S WHAT YOU ARE, JUDAS!

B-BUT YOUR HOLINESS *ASKED* ME TO DO THIS — OFFERED ME MONEY...

Inside the Palace...

I'M JESUS'S ENEMY. *YOU'RE* SUPPOSED TO BE HIS FRIEND. I NEED YOUR INFORMATION, BUT I DESPISE YOU FOR SELLING IT TO ME.

I ASSURE YOUR HOLINESS I HAVE THE HIGHEST MOTIVES...

I'M NOT INTERESTED. DOES HE SUSPECT YOU? WILL HE NOW BE ESCAPING?

N-NO, I MADE A GOOD EXCUSE FOR LEAVING. HE TRUSTS ME...

LIAR!

JESUS IS NO FOOL. WE MUST ACT QUICKLY...

The Captain of the Guard is summoned.

SIR?

CAPTAIN, TAKE YOUR MEN AND ARREST JESUS. THIS CREATURE WILL LEAD YOU TO THE PLACE.

IT'S NO GOOD HANGING ABOUT HERE — I'LL GET BACK AND WARN JESUS.

Ten minutes later.

THANK GOD! HE'S GONE. THEY'LL NEVER FIND HIM NOW.

JUDAS, WITH THE TEMPLE GUARD!

BUT THEY'VE GONE PAST! THAT CAN ONLY MEAN THAT *JUDAS KNOWS WHERE JESUS HAS GONE!*

CONTINUED

The life story of
JOHN MARK,
writer of the 2nd Gospel

A Thursday night in March, A.D.29. While Jesus and his twelve chief disciples are having supper at the house of Mark's mother, Mary of Jerusalem, Mark has been keeping watch because he knows the High Priests want to arrest Jesus secretly. One of the twelve, Judas, leaves early, and Mark trails him to the High Priests' palace. He can still hardly believe that Judas is a traitor, but when he gets back home he is relieved to find that Jesus and the others have gone. Soon, however, Mark sees Judas with the Temple Guard – and as they are *passing* the house, Judas must know where Jesus has gone!

STORY BY CHAD VARAH: DRAWN BY BELLAVITIS.

WHAT SHALL I DO? I'D SOON BE LAID OUT IF I TRIED TO STOP THEM, AND THEN THERE'D BE NO ONE TO WARN JESUS...

IT'S NO GOOD WAKING MOTHER — OH, IF ONLY MY DAD WASN'T AWAY!

I DON'T EVEN KNOW WHERE JESUS WILL BE. I'LL JUST HAVE TO FOLLOW THE GUARD...

... AND HOPE I CAN NIP AHEAD AND WARN JESUS WHEN WE GET TO THE PLACE.

EACH GO AND COLLECT HALF-A-DOZEN RESERVES, AND ASSEMBLE THEM HERE SECRETLY WITHIN AN HOUR.

AN HOUR? BUT IT WON'T TAKE...

YOU STICK TO WHAT YOU'RE PAID FOR. THERE ARE OTHER ARRANGEMENTS YOU DON'T KNOW ABOUT.

WE STAY HERE TILL WE GET A MESSAGE FROM THE HIGH PRIEST.

SAVED! JESUS WILL HAVE TIME TO GET BACK TO BETHANY!

WHAT IS IT, QUARTUS?

THE HIGH PRIEST, MY LADY.

Meanwhile, in the Roman Governor's palace, Pontius Pilate, the Governor, and his wife Claudia, are about to retire for the night.

WHAT, AT THIS TIME OF NIGHT? TELL HIM...

I'D BETTER SEE HIM, MY DEAR. WE DON'T WANT ANY TROUBLE AT THE FEAST TOMORROW.

A LATE CALL, CAIAPHAS. MAKE IT BRIEF, WILL YOU?

I'LL COME STRAIGHT TO THE POINT FOR ONCE, EXCELLENCY! CAN YOU HOLD A SPECIAL COURT AT SIX?

IF IT'S REALLY URGENT. BUT...

THERE MAY BE A RIOT AT THE FEAST UNLESS A CERTAIN AGITATOR IS EXECUTED QUICKLY. WE CAN ARREST HIM, BUT ONLY YOU CAN...

I KNOW. VERY WELL, WE NEITHER OF US WANT ANY TROUBLE. WHAT'S THE MAN'S NAME?

JESUS.

The life story of

JOHN MARK,

writer of the 2nd Gospel

A Thursday night in March, A.D.29. Jesus and his twelve chief disciples have been having a secret supper at Mark's mother's house, and Mark has been keeping watch because he knows the authorities want to arrest Jesus before the Passover festival the next day. Mark sees Judas, one of the twelve, leave early and go to the High Priests' palace. He runs back to warn Jesus who has now left. He then sees Judas with the Temple Guard, and hears them say they'll do nothing for an hour. He thinks Jesus will be safe with his friends at Bethany by then. Meanwhile, Caiaphas, the High Priest, is asking Pontius Pilate, the Roman Governor, if he will attend a special court and condemn 'an agitator' to death at six in the morning.

STORY BY CHAD VARAH:
DRAWN BY BELLAVITIS.

YOU DON'T MEAN JESUS OF NAZARETH? YOU MUST BE MAD! HE'S THE MOST POPULAR MAN IN JERUSALEM!

NEVERTHELESS...

THERE *WOULD* BE A RIOT IF WE EXECUTED *HIM*.

I ASSURE YOUR EXCELLENCY THAT NO ONE WILL LIFT A FINGER TO SAVE HIM.

AS SOON AS THEY SEE HIM POWERLESS, THEY WILL STOP BELIEVING HE IS THE CHRIST, AND TURN AGAINST HIM.

M-M-M — PERHAPS — I'M GLAD BARABBAS AND HIS BANDITS ARE SAFELY IN GAOL, THOUGH.

JESUS REFUSED *THEIR* HELP, ANYWAY.

WELL, YOU'VE MORE TO LOSE THAN I HAVE IF YOU'RE WRONG. I'LL BE IN THE PRAETORIUM AT SIX.

Meanwhile, Mark takes a short cut to make sure that Jesus is on the way to Bethany.

THANK GOD! THERE HE IS!

... BE SCATTERED. BUT AFTER I HAVE RISEN, I'LL GO BEFORE YOU INTO GALILEE.

SHOULD BE ALL RIGHT — IF THEY SCATTER TONIGHT AND JESUS GOES TO GALILEE AS SOON AS HE GETS UP TOMORROW.

I'M S'POSED TO BE IN BED. NO POINT IN GETTING SCOLDED IF THE DANGER'S PAST.

HEY, THEY'VE TURNED OFF INTO THAT GARDEN WHERE THE OLIVE VATS USED TO BE. THEY'LL BE NABBED IF THEY STAY THERE!

Mark goes forward to warn Jesus, but finds him praying.

Jesus goes on praying for a very long time.

FATHER, SPARE ME THIS — BUT THY WILL, NOT MINE, BE DONE...

CONTINUED

The life story of
JOHN MARK,
writer of the 2nd Gospel

A Thursday night in March, A.D.29. Mark knows that Jesus is going to be arrested, for one of his twelve chief followers, Judas, has promised to lead the High Priest's soldiers to a place where they can catch him away from the crowds who love him. Mark, anxious to warn Jesus, follows the soldiers and finds they mean to wait for an hour or so. He doesn't know that this is to give Caiaphas, the High Priest, time to make sure that the Roman Governor, Pilate, will hold a special Court to pass the death sentence. Mark uses the delay to look for Jesus; but when he finds him in a garden called "Gethsemane", Jesus is praying. Mark waits for him to finish, but it is nearly midnight and the boy falls asleep.

STORY BY CHAD VARAH :
DRAWN BY BELLAVITIS.

The three Jesus left on guard are asleep too . . .

PETER! JAMES! JOHN!

COULDN'T YOU WATCH FOR ONE HOUR? WATCH, AND PRAY — THE SPIRIT IS WILLING, BUT THE FLESH IS WEAK.

Meanwhile, in the Governor's Palace . . .

CLAUDIA! WHAT'S THE MATTER?

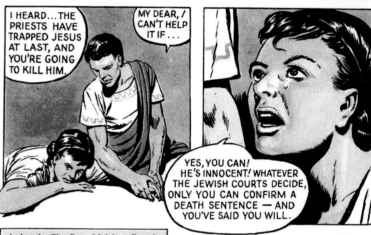

I HEARD . . . THE PRIESTS HAVE TRAPPED JESUS AT LAST, AND YOU'RE GOING TO KILL HIM.

MY DEAR, / CAN'T HELP IT IF . . .

YES, YOU CAN! HE'S INNOCENT! WHATEVER THE JEWISH COURTS DECIDE, ONLY YOU CAN CONFIRM A DEATH SENTENCE — AND YOU'VE SAID YOU WILL.

I DIDN'T KNOW YOU KNEW HIM.

MY FRIEND JOANNA'S ONE OF HIS FOLLOWERS — I WENT WITH HER ONCE TO HEAR HIM. HE'S — HE'S *GOOD*.

NO DOUBT, BUT THEY CAN GET HIM FOR BLASPHEMY FOR CLAIMING TO BE THE CHRIST.

EVEN IF HE *IS*?

And at the City Gate, Malchus, Captain of the Guard, has assembled his arrest-party and is ready to set out . . .

CAIAPHAS SAYS IT'S ALL FIXED.

ARREST-PARTY, MOVE OFF!

NOW, JUDAS, LEAD US TO THIS JESUS.

JESUS — I MUST WARN HIM — I MUST WARN . . .

Mark mutters in his sleep . . .

THE ARREST-PARTY! AND I WAS ASLEEP . . .

CONT'D

The life story of

JOHN MARK,
writer of the 2nd Gospel

Midnight on a Thursday in March, A.D.29. Mark is anxious to warn Jesus that the High Priests are sending the Temple Guard, reinforced by a gang of toughs, to arrest him, and that Judas, one of Jesus's twelve chief followers, is ready to lead the arrest-party to him. Mark follows Jesus and the other eleven disciples to a garden outside the City called "Gethsemane", but finds Jesus deep in prayer, with Peter, James and John keeping watch while the others sleep even further away. He waits for Jesus to finish praying, but at last he falls asleep. Even the men are tired, for they keep dropping off too – and when the arrest-party arrive from the City only Jesus himself has seen them approach. Mark awakes to see soldiers closing in.

STORY BY CHAD VARAH :
DRAWN BY BELLAVITIS.

RABBI! MASTER!

JUDAS!

ARREST HIM.

I'M THE MAN YOU WANT — LET THE OTHERS GO.

NO, PETER! THOSE WHO TAKE THE SWORD, DIE BY IT.

WHY DOESN'T JESUS STRIKE THEM UNCONSCIOUS, AND ESCAPE?

LET ME...

IT'S HEALED!

YOU COME WITH SWORDS AND CLUBS AS IF I WERE A BANDIT. I TAUGHT EVERY DAY IN THE TEMPLE, BUT YOU DIDN'T ARREST ME THERE. DARKNESS SUITS YOUR DARK DEED!

HA! GOT ONE OF YOU, ANYWAY!

LET ME GO!

Later.

MARK, WHATEVER...? WHY, YOU'RE CRYING, MY LOVE! DID YOU HAVE A NIGHTMARE?

I W-WISH IT WAS! THEY'VE ARRESTED JESUS, AND IT'S ALL M-MY FAULT!

CONTINUED

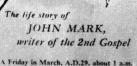

The life story of
JOHN MARK,
writer of the 2nd Gospel

A Friday in March, A.D.29, about 1 a.m.
Mark has been prevented from warning
Jesus that the Temple Guard, guided by
the traitor Judas, were coming to arrest
him. After trying all evening to see Jesus,
Mark has found him praying in a garden
outside the City, and while waiting for the
long prayer to finish has fallen asleep, and
only woken in time to see Jesus taken. The
soldiers fail to catch Peter and the
other disciples as they run away, but grab
young Mark, who is able to escape only
by wriggling out of his nightclothes. He
runs home and tells his mother (who
thought he was still safely asleep on the
flat roof of their house) that Jesus has just
been arrested and that it's all *his* fault.

STORY BY CHAD VARAH:
DRAWN BY BELLAVITIS.

JESUS ARRESTED! BUT...

I HEARD KNOCKING, MADAM, SO I GOT UP, AND... WHY, IT'S MASTER MARK!

I'M GLAD YOU WOKE — GET HIM A HOT DRINK, QUICKLY.

YES, MADAM.

NOW, TELL ME ALL ABOUT IT FROM THE BEGINNING.

WELL, MOTHER — WHEN YOU SENT ME UP TO BED, I'D BEEN TO BETHANY...

Later.

...SO ALTHOUGH I DID MY BEST TO CATCH HIM AND WARN HIM, IT WASN'T GOOD ENOUGH. HE'S MY HERO, AND I LET HIM DOWN.

NONSENSE! EXCUSE ME, MADAM, BUT WHAT LAD COULD HAVE DONE MORE? IT'S MY OPINION HE WASN'T *MEANT* TO WARN JESUS.

HE'S RIGHT, MARK. IT'S CLEAR JESUS KNEW WHAT WAS GOING TO HAPPEN, AND WAS WAITING FOR IT.

SEEMS LIKE IT — BUT WHY, WHY?

SOONER OR LATER WE JEWS HAD TO ACCEPT OR REJECT OUR CHRIST, AND THE TIME HAS COME *NOW.* WHAT WILL BE OUR CHOICE?

At the house of Annas, the former High Priest.

THESE WITNESSES ARE NO USE, ANNAS. THEY CONTRADICT ONE ANOTHER.

TAKE THEM AWAY.

QUESTION THE PRISONER ON OATH, CAIAPHAS. I'VE AN IDEA HE MAY CONDEMN HIMSELF.

BUT THAT'S ILLEGAL! H'M, I WONDER...

I CHARGE YOU BY THE LIVING GOD TO TELL US — ARE YOU THE CHRIST, THE SON OF GOD?

I AM...

YOU ALL HEARD THE BLASPHEMY — WE NEED NO OTHER WITNESSES! WHAT DO YOU THINK?

GUILTY. HE MUST DIE.

CONTINUED

The life story of

JOHN MARK,

writer of the 2nd Gospel

A Friday in March, A.D.29, in the small hours of the morning, Mark has seen Jesus arrested by the Temple Guard, led to him by the traitor Judas, and has only escaped being seized himself by wriggling out of his nightclothes. He has run home, exhausted, cold, and heartbroken, blaming himself for having failed to warn Jesus in time. His mother comforts him with a hot drink and the assurance that Jesus must have known his danger and waited for arrest in order to force the people to accept him as the Christ, or reject him. The High Priests hold a preliminary trial but their witnesses contradict one another, so Caiaphas illegally makes Jesus condemn himself on oath – for when he admits he claims to be the Christ, that is taken as blasphemy, for which the penalty is death.

STORY BY CHAD VARAH: DRAWN BY BELLAVITIS.

AWAY WITH THE BLASPHEMER!

PROPHESY, YOU "CHRIST"! WHO JUST HIT YOU?

HAVE YOU SUMMONED THE SANHEDRIN COUNCIL, CAIAPHAS?

YES, ANNAS—THEY'LL MEET AT DAWN. AND THEY'LL CONFIRM OUR VERDICT, NEVER FEAR!

Meanwhile, Mark is put to bed . . .

YOU CAN GET UP AS EARLY AS YOU LIKE, BUT YOU MUST SLEEP NOW.

CAN'T DO —ANY MORE— NOW—FIND OUT. —'MORROW...

OH, YOU'RE THE FISH-CHAP —WANT TO SEE THE COOK? COME IN.

THANK YOU.

I'LL FIND OUT WHAT'S HAPPENING. STAY BY THE FIRE.

HOPE I'M NOT RECOGNIZED...

At the gate of Annas's courtyard, John and Peter have followed the arrest-party at a distance.

YOU WERE WITH JESUS, TOO.

I DON'T KNOW WHAT YOU'RE TALKING ABOUT.

OCK-A-DOODLE-OO!

FIRST COCKCROW. NIGHT'S GETTING ON.

WEREN'T YOU SCARED, ARRESTING THE MIRACLE-WORKER?

NOT ME. BUT IT WAS DANGEROUS, MIND.

HE HAS STRANGE POWERS. AND A DOZEN GALILEANS WITH HIM.

I RECKON THIS IS ONE OF 'EM.

NO, I'M NOT.

WELL, YOU'VE A GALILEAN ACCENT— AND I THINK I SAW YOU IN THE GARDEN WITH HIM.

DRAT AND BLAST YOU, I DON'T EVEN KNOW THE MAN!

OCK—A-DOODLE-OO!

THE COCK! JESUS TOLD ME, "BEFORE SECOND COCKCROW, YOU'LL DENY ME THREE TIMES!" AND I SWORE I'D DIE WITH HIM FIRST!

HE LOOKED AT ME AS THEY BROUGHT HIM OUT! HE *KNEW!* OH, GOD HELP ME—I'M WORSE THAN JUDAS!

CONTINUED

The life story of
JOHN MARK,
writer of the 2nd Gospel

A Friday in March, A.D.29, in the small hours of the morning, Mark has had a terrible day, trying in vain to warn Jesus of the danger gathering round him, and narrowly escaping being arrested with him. Mark's mother comforts him with the assurance that Jesus knew of the plot against him and refused to run away. She puts her son to bed, telling him no boy could have done more, and saying he may get up as soon as he wakes, to find out what is happening. Meanwhile, Jesus has been condemned by Caiaphas and Annas (the present and former High Priests), and handed to the soldiers to be mocked and bullied until the full Council (the "Sanhedrin") can meet, and pass sentence. Peter, skulking outside in the courtyard, has denied that he knows Jesus — and finds Jesus looking at him as the soldiers drag him away. "I'm worse than the traitor Judas!" sobs Peter.

STORY BY CHAD VARAH : DRAWN BY BELLAVITIS.

IF HE WERE *REALLY* THE CHRIST, HE'D STRIKE 'EM ALL DEAD AND ESCAPE!

WE ALL FAILED HIM — AND I...

CHRIST CAME TO SAVE MEN, NOT TO DESTROY THEM.

COME, PETER.

I DENIED HIM, JOHN...

STOP THAT. GO AND TELL JOSEPH OF ARIMATHEA WHAT'S HAPPENED. I'LL TELL NICODEMUS. THEY'RE BOTH ON THE SANHEDRIN COUNCIL. HURRY!

While Jerusalem sleeps, unconscious of the events of the night, the chief actors in the drama are awake...

Annas and Caiaphas.

THE SANHEDRIN WILL CONDEMN JESUS FOR BLASPHEMY, BUT WHAT DOES PILATE CARE ABOUT THAT?

HE WON'T *HEAR* THE CASE — HE'LL JUST SIGN THE DEATH-WARRANT.

Pilate and Claudia.

YOU'RE A ROMAN—YOU *CAN'T* CONDEMN AN INNOCENT MAN!

MY DEAR, I'VE TOLD YOU I'LL INSIST ON A PROPER TRIAL. NOW LET'S GET SOME SLEEP!

Judas.

WHAT HAVE I DONE? OH, WHAT HAVE I DONE? WHAT HAVE I DONE...

A gang of Jewish 'Underground Forces'.

IF PILATE OFFERS TO FREE A PRISONER, WE SHOUT FOR OUR LEADER, BARABBAS.

AND IF ANYONE SHOUTS FOR JESUS, COSH HIM.

GET ALL YOUR PALS TO YELL "CRUCIFY JESUS", AND THEY'LL BE PAID THE SAME. ORDERS OF THE HIGH PRIEST.

Local tramps and idlers.

COUNT ON US, GUV.

Councillors Joseph and Nicodemus.

IT'S A PUT-UP JOB. I SHALL VOTE AGAINST THE DEATH PENALTY, JOSEPH.

I'VE TRIED TO KEEP MY ADMIRATION FOR JESUS SECRET UP TO NOW, BUT — HE SHALL HAVE MY VOTE, TOO.

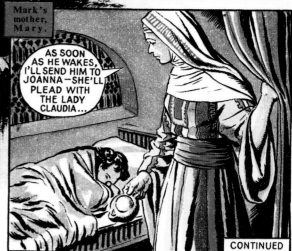

Mark's mother, Mary.

AS SOON AS HE WAKES, I'LL SEND HIM TO JOANNA—SHE'LL PLEAD WITH THE LADY CLAUDIA...

CONTINUED

The life story of
JOHN MARK,
writer of the 2nd Gospel

A Friday in March, A.D.29. Dawn. Mark is asleep after a frightening day of trying to warn Jesus of the plot against him, and nearly being arrested with him. Jesus, betrayed by one disciple, denied by another, and forsaken by all the rest except John, is in the hands of the High Priests, who are determined to have him put to death before the Jewish pilgrims who throng Jerusalem for the Passover-Feast can proclaim him King. Caiaphas has called the Sanhedrin, the Supreme Council of the Jews, to meet and condemn Jesus for "blasphemy" in claiming to be the Christ promised by God; and he has arranged for the Roman Governor, Pontius Pilate, to sentence him to death. A number of agitators have been paid to shout "Crucify Jesus", and if all goes according to plan it will be too late to save him by the time the common people know what's happening. But Mark's mother knows a friend of Pilate's wife . . .

STORY BY CHAD VARAH: DRAWN BY BELLAVITIS.

WUH-WAH—OH, IT'S YOU, MUM—WHAT'S THE TIME?

FIVE. I HATE TO DISTURB YOU, DARLING—YOU'RE SO TIRED...

I'M ALL RIGHT, MOTHER—SLEPT LIKE A LOG. IS THERE—ANY NEWS?

NO, BUT I'VE THOUGHT OF A WAY OF HELPING JESUS.

I'LL DO ANYTHING...

I WANT YOU TO GET INTO HEROD'S PALACE WITHOUT BEING NOTICED, AND GO TO THE ROOMS OF HIS STEWARD, CHUZA.

I CAN DO THAT—THAT'S BETTER—BUT WHY?

BECAUSE HIS WIFE, JOANNA, IS NOT ONLY "ONE OF US"—SHE'S ALSO THE FRIEND OF THE LADY CLAUDIA.

PILATE'S WIFE! IF JOANNA CAN GET HER TO PERSUADE PILATE NOT TO SENTENCE JESUS...LEAVE IT TO ME, MOTHER!

At Herod's Palace . . .

I'LL CARRY THAT ONE IN FOR YOU.

THANK'EE, LAD—IT'S A BIT AWKWARD.

HERE'S THE MILK AT LAST. A BOWL OF IT FOR CHUZA, PLEASE.

OH, ALL RIGHT. HAVEN'T SEEN YOU BEFORE—ARE YOU NEW?

VERY.

LOST MY WAY—WHICH IS THE STEWARD'S BEDROOM, PLEASE?

CAN'T YOU HEAR HIM SNORING?

JOANNA! PSSSST! JOANNA!

SH! WHAT IS IT? AREN'T YOU JOHN MARK, MARY'S SON?

YES. MOTHER SENT ME TO TELL YOU JESUS HAS BEEN ARRESTED...

Meanwhile, at the Sanhedrin-Council . . .

GUILTY!

GUILTY!

GUILTY!

JOSEPH! WE'RE OUT-VOTED! JESUS IS CONDEMNED!

CONTINUED

The life story of JOHN MARK, writer of the 2nd Gospel

A Friday in March, A.D.29, about 5.30 a.m. Jesus, the Galilean prophet believed by many Jews to be their promised "Christ" (Divine King), has been betrayed by one of his own disciples, Judas, to the High Priests, who want him out of the way before the Passover Festival. They have condemned him to death for "blasphemy" and the Sanhedrin-Council has confirmed their verdict, only Councillors Nicodemus and Joseph of Arimathea disagreeing. The sentence must be approved by the Roman Governor, Pontius Pilate, who has agreed to hold a special Court at 6.0. Meanwhile, young Mark has found out what is going on and has wangled his way into Herod's palace to tell Joanna, the Steward's wife, who is a believer in Jesus and is a friend of Pilate's wife, the Lady Claudia Procula. Mark and his mother hope Joanna will persuade Claudia to tell Pilate that Jesus is the victim of a conspiracy . . .

STORY BY CHAD VARAH: DRAWN BY BELLAVITIS.

I'M SO GLAD YOU LET ME KNOW. IF ONLY WE'RE IN TIME!

GOOD MORNING, MADAM.

WE *MUST* BE. IF PILATE'S GONE...

I'M AFRAID THE LADY CLAUDIA ISN'T UP YET IF MADAM WOULD CARE TO WAIT . . .

IT'S VERY URGENT. I'LL GO UP — I KNOW THE WAY.

PLEASE, SIR, HAS THE GOVERNOR LEFT YET?

YES — OH DEAR, I HOPE MY LADY WON'T BE ANNOYED . . .

CLAUDIA, WHAT IS IT?

I'VE HAD SUCH A BAD DREAM. VOICES — IN EVERY LANGUAGE — OVER AND OVER — THEY WOULDN'T STOP — HORRIBLE...

BUT WHAT DID THEY *SAY*?

THEY SAID "JESUS — CRUCIFIED — UNDER PONTIUS PILATE" — MY HUSBAND!

IT NEEDN'T HAPPEN. YOU MUST STOP IT. THERE'S STILL TIME.

HE PROMISED TO GIVE JESUS A FAIR TRIAL . . .

GOOD. BUT YOU MUST TELL HIM ABOUT YOUR DREAM.

HE'S GONE, BUT I'LL WRITE A MESSAGE AND SEND A MAN WITH IT NOW.

NOT A SOLDIER — SOME OFFICER MIGHT MAKE HIM WAIT TILL AFTER THE TRIAL. I'LL FETCH YOUNG MARK.

THIS IS MARK, ALSO A DISCIPLE OF JESUS. HE SPEAKS GREEK QUITE WELL, BUT NOT MUCH LATIN.

WE NEED YOUR HELP, MARK.

I'LL DO ANYTHING FOR JESUS AND — AND YOU, MY LADY.

THEN GET THIS MESSAGE TO MY HUSBAND QUICKLY. DON'T LET ANYONE STOP YOU. IT MAY MAKE ALL THE DIFFERENCE.

CONTINUED

MARK THE YOUNGEST DISCIPLE

The life story of **JOHN MARK**, *writer of the 2nd Gospel*

STORY BY CHAD VARAH : DRAWN BY BELLAVITIS.

A Friday in March, A.D.29, about 6 a.m. Jesus, the Galilean prophet believed by many Jews to be their promised "Christ" (Divine King), has been betrayed by Judas to the High Priests. They have condemned him to death for "blasphemy", and the Sanhedrin-Council has confirmed their verdict, only Councillors Nicodemus and Joseph of Arimathea disagreeing. The sentence must be approved by the Roman Governor, Pontius Pilate, who has agreed to hold a Court at 6.0. Meanwhile, Mark has reached Herod's palace to tell Joanna, the Steward's wife, who is a believer in Jesus and a friend of Pilate's wife, the Lady Claudia Procula. Mark and his mother hope Joanna will persuade Claudia to tell Pilate that Jesus is the victim of a conspiracy. Joanna and Mark arrive at the Governor's Palace after Pilate has left, but Joanna gets the Lady Claudia to write a message for Mark to take to the Praetorium, where the Court is held. Claudia tells Mark not to let anyone stop him.

THERE GOES MARK! PRAY GOD HE'S IN TIME.

PRAY GOD MY HUSBAND TAKES NOTICE! THAT AWFUL DREAM...

AT LAST I CAN DO SOMETHING THAT WILL *REALLY* HELP JESUS...

Meanwhile, at the High Priests' Palace . . .

TAKE THE PRISONER TO PILATE.

NO!

JUDAS! WHY, YOU...

I—I DIDN'T KNOW—THEY'D K-KILL HIM...

IT WAS OBVIOUS, YOU TRAITOR!

I'VE SINNED, CAIAPHAS! I'VE BETRAYED AN INNOCENT MAN!

THAT'S YOUR LOOK-OUT — NOTHING TO DO WITH US.

HE'LL KILL HIMSELF. WELL, HE'S SERVED HIS PURPOSE.

BLOOD-MONEY — PITY WE CAN'T PUT IT INTO TEMPLE FUNDS...

Later, on the steps of the Praetorium.

HERE'S THE PRISONER, SIR. JESUS, FROM NAZARETH IN GALILEE.

RIGHT. WE'LL TAKE OVER. YOU CAN GO.

AREN'T YOU GOING IN TOO, SIR?

WHAT, ENTER A HEATHEN BUILDING WHEN WE'RE PURIFIED FOR A FEAST?

HIS EXCELLENCY PROMISED TO COME OUT TO US. HE'S NOT *HEARING* THE CASE — ONLY PASSING SENTENCE. CRUCIFIXION!

CONTINUED

The life story of
JOHN MARK,
writer of the 2nd Gospel

A Friday in March, A.D.29, about 6.15 a.m. Jesus has been betrayed by Judas, one of his own disciples, and condemned by the High Priests, Annas and Caiaphas, for "blasphemy" in claiming to be the promised "Christ" (Divine King of the Jews). The Sanhedrin-Council has confirmed the sentence, and Pontius Pilate, the Roman Governor, has promised to impose the death penalty. When Judas realizes this, he flings his blood-money back at the Priests and goes off to hang himself. Jesus is taken to the Praetorium to be judged by Pilate, and Caiaphas is sure the Governor won't bother to hear the case. He doesn't know that Pilate's wife, the Lady Claudia, admires Jesus, or that her friend Joanna is a disciple and has got her to write a letter to her husband. Mark is given this letter to take quickly to Pilate . . .

STORY BY CHAD VARAH: DRAWN BY BELLAVITIS.

HEY, LAD! JUST A MINUTE!

SORRY, SIR — I'M IN A HURRY.

WHAT, IN TOO MUCH OF A HURRY TO EARN *THIS?* SILVER, MY BOY!

WH-WHAT DID YOU WANT ME TO DO?

THAT'S BETTER! THE EARLY BIRD CATCHES THE WORM! ALL YOU HAVE TO DO IS TO STAY A BIT AND WHEN I GIVE THE SIGNAL . . .

. . . SHOUT "CRUCIFY HIM!"

C-CRUCIFY WHOM, SIR?

JESUS!

I WOULDN'T SHOUT FOR *ANYONE* TO BE TORTURED TO DEATH. LET ME GO!

OH? YOU TALK LIKE A FRIEND OF HIS...

HERE COMES PILATE NOW, BOSS! BETTER BE READY!

CAN'T GO UP THERE, SONNY!

BUT I HAVE A MESSAGE FOR THE GOVERNOR!

THE LADY CLAUDIA WANTS HIM TO HAVE IT BEFORE HE PASSES SENTENCE.

SO HE SHALL, IF YOU BEHAVE YOURSELF. SHUT UP AND LISTEN.

WHAT ACCUSATION DO YOU BRING AGAINST THE PRISONER?

THAT'S THE FORMAL OPENING OF A ROMAN TRIAL. THE GOVERNOR'S HEARING THE CASE AFTER ALL — AND IF YOU ASK ME, JESUS WILL GET OFF!

CONTINUED

The life story of
JOHN MARK,
writer of the 2nd Gospel

A Friday in March, A.D.29, about 6.15 a.m. Jesus has been condemned by the High Priests and the Jewish Council for "blasphemy" in claiming to be the Christ. Annas and his son-in-law Caiaphas, the High Priests, are sure that Pontius Pilate, the Roman Governor, will confirm the death-sentence without hearing the case. They don't know that Pilate's wife, the Lady Claudia, admires Jesus and has made her husband promise to give Jesus a fair trial. Her bosom friend Joanna, a follower of Jesus, has got her to write a further appeal to Pilate, and sent it by Mark with instructions to get it to Pilate quickly. Mark is held up by an agent of the High Priest who is bribing people to shout for Jesus to be killed, and is stopped by a Roman officer just as the trial begins. The officer thinks Jesus will get off.

STORY BY CHAD VARAH : DRAWN BY BELLAVITIS.

YOU SAID HE WOULDN'T HEAR THE CASE, CAIAPHAS!

PILATE WON'T CARE ABOUT BLASPHEMY. WHAT CAN WE SAY?

IF HE WEREN'T A CRIMINAL, WE WOULDN'T HAVE BROUGHT HIM TO YOU!

H'M . . .

TAKE HIM, THEN, AND JUDGE HIM BY YOUR OWN LAWS.

BUT WE AREN'T ALLOWED TO *EXECUTE* ANYONE. HE MUST DIE!

HE'S GUILTY BY *YOUR* LAW — FORBIDDING PEOPLE TO PAY TAXES TO CAESAR AND SAYING HE'S A KING HIMSELF.

NOT A BAD EFFORT ON THE SPUR OF THE MOMENT. THE GOVERNOR'S GOING IN TO QUESTION JESUS ABOUT IT.

ARE YOU A KING?

I AM. BUT MY KINGDOM IS NOT OF THIS WORLD. IF IT WERE, MY SERVANTS WOULD FIGHT FOR ME.

AS YOU HEAR, THEY'RE ACCUSING YOU OF ALL SORTS OF THINGS. AREN'T YOU GOING TO DEFEND YOURSELF?

YOU SCORN TO ANSWER THEM.

I CAME INTO THE WORLD TO TEACH TRUTH. ONLY THOSE WHO LOVE TRUTH WILL LISTEN TO ME.

TRUTH? AH, BUT WHAT *IS* TRUTH?

SILENCE FOR THE GOVERNOR!

HE'S BACK — CAN I GIVE HIM THE MESSAGE NOW?

I HAVE EXAMINED THE ACCUSED. I FIND NO FAULT IN HIM AT ALL. HE IS NOT GUILTY.

CONTINUED

The life story of
JOHN MARK,
writer of the 2nd Gospel

Mark has been entrusted with a vital letter. His hero, the young prophet Jesus, has been arrested by the Jewish authorities and condemned by the High Priests and the "Sanhedrin" (Council) for "blasphemy" in claiming to be the promised Christ. The penalty is death, but only the Roman Governor, Pontius Pilate, can pass sentence. Caiaphas, the High Priest, has arranged for this by describing Jesus as a dangerous agitator who must be executed before the Passover festival begins. He doesn't know that Pilate's wife, the Lady Claudia, has begged her husband to give Jesus a fair trial instead of simply passing sentence; or that her friend Joanna, a follower of Jesus, has persuaded her to send Pilate a written message to be carried by Mark. Mark is waiting for an opportunity to give the Governor this letter, when Pilate announces that he has examined Jesus and finds him NOT GUILTY.

STORY BY CHAD VARAH. DRAWN BY BELLAVITIS.

NOT GUILTY?

HURRAY!

BUT HE'S BEEN STIRRING UP THE PEOPLE, RIGHT FROM GALILEE TO HERE!

THE LETTER WON'T MATTER NOW. BUT I PROMISED TO SEE THAT THE GOVERNOR GOT IT—WILL YOU GIVE IT TO HIM WHILE I RUN BACK WITH THE NEWS?

YES, FIRST CHANCE I GET.

RELEASE A PRISONER, PILATE!

IT'S PASSOVER TIME—REMEMBER THE CUSTOM!

RELEASE A PRISONER!

BETTER STILL! THEY'LL SHOUT FOR JESUS—HE'S SO POPULAR...

BUT YOUR EXCELLENCY PROMISED! OUR COUNCIL HAS CONDEMNED THE MAN, AND...

TO SAVE YOUR FACES, I'LL HAVE HIM WHIPPED BEFORE LETTING HIM GO.

WHAT, WHEN WE'VE SAID HE DESERVES DEATH? YOU ROMANS USE US TO KEEP OUR NATION IN ORDER, AND YOU SHOULD BACK US UP!

LETTER FROM THE LADY CLAUDIA PROCULA, SIR. CAME JUST BEFORE THE TRIAL.

"DON'T DO ANYTHING TO THAT GOOD MAN. I'VE HAD TERRIBLE DREAMS ABOUT HIM AND YOU."

AS USUAL AT PASSOVER, I SHALL SET FREE A PRISONER. CHOOSE—THE BANDIT-CHIEF, BARABBAS—OR JESUS, CALLED "CHRIST"?

CONTINUED

The life story of
JOHN MARK,
writer of the 2nd Gospel

Jesus has been arrested and condemned for "blasphemy" by the Jewish authorities, but cannot be put to death unless Pontius Pilate, the Roman Governor, agrees. Caiaphas, the High Priest, is sure he will have no trouble with Pilate, not knowing that the Governor's wife, Lady Claudia, has made her husband promise to give Jesus a fair trial. Furthermore, Claudia's friend Joanna, a follower of Jesus, has got her to write a message to Pilate and send it by Mark. Mark can't give Pilate the message before the trial begins, and when Pilate declares Jesus "Not Guilty", Mark leaves the letter with a Roman officer and returns to Claudia and Joanna. Pilate has trouble with Caiaphas about the verdict when he gets the letter, so he stands at the Judgment Seat on Gabbatha Pavement and says he will free a prisoner to celebrate the Festival—will they have the bandit Barabbas, or Jesus?

STORY BY CHAD VARAH : DRAWN BY BELLAVITIS.

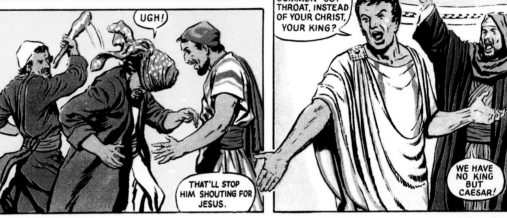

CONTINUED

The life story of JOHN MARK, writer of the 2nd Gospel

Jesus has been condemned by the Jewish authorities for claiming to be the Christ, but found innocent by the Roman Governor of Judaea, Pontius Pilate, who alone can impose the death penalty. Pilate has been urged by his wife, both personally and in a letter brought to the Praetorium by Mark, to give Jesus a fair trial. He has done so; but the High Priest, Caiaphas, won't accept the verdict, and Pilate has the idea of offering to set free either Jesus or a bandit called Barabbas, as it was the custom to release one prisoner at Passover-time. The crowd, which consists largely of Barabbas's gangsters and of people bribed by the Priests, chooses Barabbas - and Mark returns from taking Pilate's wife the good news of the verdict to hear the crowd yelling for Jesus to be crucified. A Roman officer tells him that Pilate's chief duty is to avoid a riot among the Jews.

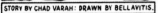
STORY BY CHAD VARAH: DRAWN BY BELLAVITIS.

KILL HIM! CRUCIFY HIM!

NOT WHEN I'VE FOUND HIM INNOCENT. TO SATISFY YOUR COUNCIL, I'LL HAVE HIM FLOGGED BEFORE I LET HIM GO.

SEE TO IT, OFFICER. THEN SHOW HIM TO THE CROWD. BRING BARABBAS OUT AT THE SAME TIME.

RIGHT, SIR.

BUT A ROMAN FLOGGING NEARLY KILLS A MAN — OUCH!

A few minutes later.

THE USUAL THIRTY-NINE STROKES. READY?

Soon...

THAT'S THE LOT. CUT HIM DOWN.

YES, SIR.

H'M, TOOK IT WITHOUT A MURMUR— NEVER KNOWN THAT HAPPEN BEFORE!

AH, BECAUSE HE SAYS HE'S A KING, SEE?

THEN LET'S DRESS 'IM UP AS ONE. WE CAN MAKE A CROWN OF THORNS...

LOOK AT THE MAN!

FLOGGING'S NOT ENOUGH. CRUCIFY HIM!

CRUCIFY HIM!

CRUCIFY HIM YOURSELVES — HE'S INNOCENT BY ROMAN LAW.

YOU KNOW WE CAN'T. BUT BY OUR LAW HE OUGHT TO DIE. HE SAYS HE'S THE SON OF GOD!

WHO ARE YOU? WHERE DO YOU COME FROM?

DON'T LOOK AT ME LIKE THAT! ANSWER ME! I'VE POWER TO CRUCIFY YOU OR LET YOU GO, YOU KNOW!

YOU HAVE THE POWER GOD LETS YOU HAVE. MY ACCUSER'S SIN IS GREATER THAN YOURS.

IF YOU LET THIS "KING" GO, YOU'RE NO FRIEND OF CAESAR'S!

CONTINUED

The life story of
JOHN MARK,
writer of the 2nd Gospel

Mark's hero, Jesus, has been condemned by the Jewish authorities for claiming to be the Christ, but Pontius Pilate, the Roman Governor, has been urged by his wife to hear the case, and has found Jesus innocent. The High Priest, Caiaphas, quarrels with the verdict, and Pilate offers the crowd the choice of a prisoner to be set free. Bribed and intimidated by the priests' agents and by "Zealot" bandits, the crowd shouts for Barabbas, the bandit leader, and calls for Jesus to be crucified. To Mark's horror, Pilate staves off a riot by ordering Jesus to be flogged. Mark doesn't know that Pilate is hoping the crowd will be satisfied when they see Jesus half-dead after 39 lashes. Jesus takes the scourging without a murmur, and the Roman soldiers dress him up in mock-royal style and show him to the vast crowd of Jews. They still yell "Crucify him!" and Caiaphas tells Pilate that it would be disloyal to Caesar to let "King" Jesus go free.

STORY BY CHAD VARAH : DRAWN BY BELLAVITIS .

WHAT ARE YOU DOING HERE?

BRING JESUS AND BARABBAS TO THE JUDGMENT SEAT.

ANYONE WHO CLAIMS TO BE A KING IS DEFYING CAESAR'S AUTHORITY, PILATE!

RIGHT, SIR.

GET BACK INTO THE CROWD!

OUCH! STEADY!

SORRY, NICODEMUS, SIR!

YOU COULDN'T HELP IT. THESE ROMANS DO AS THEY LIKE—WE'RE A CONQUERED PEOPLE.

IF YOU'RE SO FOND OF CAESAR, CAIAPHAS, ACCEPT THE VERDICT OF HIS PROCURATOR, PILATE!

STAND UP FOR YOUR OWN PEOPLE FOR A CHANGE!

JESUS IS INNOCENT!

SHUT UP, YOU, OR I'LL BREAK YOUR NECK!

WHICH SHALL I SET FREE, JESUS OR BARABBAS?

BARABBAS!

Barabbas is set free.

AND WHAT OF JESUS, YOUR "CHRIST"? LOOK AT HIM!

CRUCIFY HIM!

WHAT, CRUCIFY YOUR KING?

WE HAVE NO KING BUT CAESAR!

CENTURION! TAKE CHARGE OF THE EXECUTION. AND SEND ME A BOWL OF WATER. JUMP TO IT!

RIGHT, SIR.

I AM INNOCENT OF THE BLOOD OF THAT JUST MAN. I WASH MY HANDS OF IT!

COUNCILLOR NICODEMUS! THEY — THEY'RE GOING TO KILL JESUS!

I VOTED AGAINST IT. THERE'S NOTHING MORE ANY OF US CAN DO NOW.

CONTINUED

The life story of
JOHN MARK,
writer of the 2nd Gospel

A Friday in March A.D.29, about 8 a.m. Mark's hero, Jesus, the young prophet from Nazareth, has been condemned to death by the religious leaders of his own people, the Jews, for claiming to be the promised Christ – the King sent by God. The Roman Governor, Pontius Pilate, isn't interested in "blasphemy", so the High Priest, Caiaphas, accuses Jesus of conspiring against Caesar (the Roman Emperor). Pilate has been urged by his wife Claudia, both personally and in a letter carried by Mark, to give Jesus a fair trial, and finds him innocent. But the priests get the mob to riot, and at last Pilate gives in to them. First he has Jesus cruelly flogged; and when this doesn't satisfy the mob, he agrees to Jesus being executed by being nailed to a cross and left to die. He calls for water and washes his hands of the whole business. Mark is horrified when he realizes that Jesus, though not guilty, is to be crucified; but Councillor Nicodemus (one of the two who voted against the death penalty) tells him there is nothing more to be done.

STORY BY CHAD VARAH : DRAWN BY BELLAVITIS.

BUT THERE *MUST* BE SOMETHING WE CAN DO!

NO, MARK. ONLY A MIRACLE CAN SAVE HIM NOW—AND HE WON'T PERFORM ONE TO SAVE HIMSELF.

As the soldiers clear the space before The Judgment Seat and bring out the crosses, the mob falls silent.

IF ONLY I WERE A MAN, I'D LEAD A PARTY TO RESCUE HIM!

HE WOULDN'T WANT THAT. HIS PEOPLE HAVE REJECTED HIM. NOTHING CAN ALTER THAT NOW.

BUT IT'S BETTER TO LIVE THAN TO DIE!

JESUS WOULD SAY "IT'S BETTER TO DIE FOR WHAT YOU BELIEVE, THAN TO SAVE YOURSELF BY GIVING IT UP".

THERE ARE THREE MEN TO BE EXECUTED, SIR. I'VE WRITTEN THE PLACARDS FOR THE TWO ROBBERS, BUT...

GIVE ME THE ONE FOR JESUS.

DON'T WRITE "THE KING OF THE JEWS", BUT THAT HE *SAID* "I AM THE K ..."

WHAT I'VE WRITTEN, I'VE WRITTEN!

PUT HIS OWN CLOTHES ON HIM BEFORE HE STARTS CARRYING HIS CROSS. AND GET THE OTHER TWO LINED UP.

YES, SIR.

HE'S DOWN! JESUS HAS FALLEN!

MAKE HIM GET UP AGAIN, THEN!

I'M NOT GOING BACK TO LADY CLAUDIA! PILATE CAN TELL HER HIMSELF WHAT HE'S DONE!

GO TO YOUR MOTHER, MY BOY. YOU DID *YOUR* BEST.

At Mark's home . . .

JESUS WAS ALWAYS LOVING TO EVERYBODY. HOW *COULD* THEY DO SUCH HORRIBLE THINGS TO HIM, MOTHER?

EVIL MEN HATE GOODNESS.

BUT WHY DO THEY ALWAYS *WIN* ? IN A FEW HOURS JESUS WILL BE DEAD, AND THEY'LL HAVE BEATEN HIM.

I WONDER...

YOU MEAN — HE RAISED LAZARUS FROM THE DEAD —MOTHER, YOU DON'T MEAN THAT HE HIMSELF...? NO, IT ISN'T POSSIBLE!

CONTINUED

The life story of
JOHN MARK,
writer of the 2nd Gospel

A Friday in March, A.D. 29, about 9.0 a.m. Mark's hero, Jesus, has been condemned by the Jewish Sanhedrin-Council for "blasphemy" in claiming to be the Christ sent by God, found "not guilty" of rebellion against Caesar by the Roman Governor, Pontius Pilate, but nevertheless flogged and taken away to be killed by crucifixion in order to satisfy the priests and the mob who support them. Mark, who has taken a letter from the Lady Claudia to her husband, Pilate, pleading for fair play for Jesus, is so horrified by the Governor's weakness that he goes home to his mother instead of returning to tell Claudia what has happened. Mark asks his mother why evil should triumph over good. Why should wicked men be able to defeat and kill a man like Jesus! Mary wonders if Jesus *will* be defeated by death. Mark, remembering that Jesus raised Lazarus from the dead, says surely she can't mean that Jesus himself could come back from the grave . . .

STORY BY CHAD VARAH. DRAWN BY BELLAVITIS.

MOTHER, I'VE JUST THOUGHT OF SOMETHING! LAST NIGHT, WHEN I WAS TRYING TO WARN JESUS — WAS IT ONLY LAST NIGHT? — IT SEEMS SO LONG AGO . . .

IN THE GARDEN OF GETHSEMANE, WHEN YOU WERE NEARLY ARRESTED TOO, YOU MEAN?

NO, BEFORE THAT! ON THE WAY TO THE GARDEN, I OVER-HEARD JESUS SAY :

. . . BE SCATTERED. BUT AFTER I HAVE RISEN, I'LL GO BEFORE YOU INTO GALILEE.

I THOUGHT HE MEANT HE'D ESCAPE TO GALILEE WHEN HE GOT UP IN THE MORNING. BUT SUPPOSE "RISEN" MEANT "RISEN FROM THE DEAD"?

BUT EVEN IF IT DOES, THAT DOESN'T ALTER WHAT THEY'VE DONE TO HIM — WHAT THEY'RE DOING AT THIS MOMENT . . .

On Skull Hill.

NOW THE OTHER ONE, READY?

FATHER, FORGIVE THEM — THEY KNOW NOT WHAT THEY DO . . .

Three hours later, at noon, darkness falls on Jerusalem.

At 3.0 p.m. . . . .

THAT AWFUL DARKNESS IS LIFTING AT LAST — D'YOU KNOW, I THINK HE DIED AFTER SHOUTING "IT IS FINISHED!"

WE CAN SOON MAKE SURE !

At dusk, Pilate still hasn't gone home.

YES, SIR, HE DIED ABOUT THREE. I EXAMINED THE BODY MYSELF.

THEN COUNCILLOR JOSEPH HERE CAN TAKE IT FOR BURIAL.

Joanna, Mary Magdalene, and another Mary watch Nicodemus help Joseph to put the body in Joseph's own new tomb.

JUST A MINUTE, SIR! WE'VE TO SEAL THE TOMB AND GUARD IT. ORDERS OF THE HIGH PRIEST.

CONTINUED

SO EVEN CAIAPHAS WONDERS IF JESUS WILL RISE AGAIN . . .

The life story of
JOHN MARK,
writer of the 2nd Gospel

Mark's hero, Jesus, the young prophet from Nazareth whom many people believed to be the Divine King promised by God, has been put to death by crucifixion, after the religious leaders have rejected him and persuaded the Roman Governor to have him executed even though he was innocent by Roman law. Mark is in despair until his mother doubts whether Jesus can be defeated even by death. Then Mark remembers how Jesus raised Lazarus from the dead, and how he himself overheard Jesus tell the disciples on the way to the Garden of Gethsemane that after he had "risen", he would go to Galilee. Mark watches the body of Jesus being buried by Nicodemus and Joseph of Arimathea in Joseph's new tomb. He sees some of the Temple Guard, led by Malchus, come to the grave, and tell Joseph that the High Priest has ordered them to seal and guard the tomb. So it looks to Mark as if Caiaphas is also wondering if death is the end of Jesus . . .

STORY BY CHAD VARAH : DRAWN BY BELLAVITIS.

YES, THAT'S THE RIGHT BODY. YOU CAN CLOSE THE TOMB NOW, AND I'LL SEAL IT.

WHAT DO YOU MEAN, "THE RIGHT BODY"?

NOW FOR THE MORTAR — WHY? OH, THE HIGH PRIEST THINKS JESUS'S FRIENDS MIGHT HIDE THE BODY AND PRETEND HE'S RISEN AGAIN.

CAIAPHAS IS A FOOL. JESUS HATED LIES, AND HIS FRIENDS WOULD NEVER DO SUCH A THING.

SIR, DO YOU THINK JESUS *WILL* RISE AGAIN?

I WISH I COULD BELIEVE HE WOULD, MY BOY. BUT I CAN'T...

Two days later, at dawn . . .

"THE THIRD DAY", JESUS SAID. THAT'S TODAY. GLAD I WOKE EARLY — WHAT A LOVELY BRIGHT MORNING!

HEY, WHAT'S ALL THE COMMOTION AT THIS EARLY HOUR? I'LL NIP DOWN AND SEE.

HAVE YOU COME FROM THE TOMB? HAS JESUS RISEN? WHAT HAPPENED?

OUT OF MY WAY, BOY!

PLEASE TELL ME — I SAW YOU SEAL THE TOMB...

THE SEAL WAS UNBROKEN — BUT *HE* PASSED BY ME — WE ROLLED BACK THE STONE — THE BODY WAS GONE!

A few minutes later . . .

IT'S TRUE! HE'S RISEN! HE'S ALIVE!

HOW CAN WE EMBALM THE BODY IF WE CAN'T GET INTO THE TOMB? THAT HEAVY STONE...

Mary Magdalene, Salome and another Mary come to embalm the body.

LOOK! IT'S BEEN MOVED! THE TOMB'S OPEN!

CONTINUED

The life story of
JOHN MARK,
writer of the 2nd Gospel

Jesus has been crucified, even though the Roman Governor has found him innocent. His body has been buried by the two Jewish Councillors who voted against the death penalty, Nicodemus and Joseph of Arimathea, in the latter's own new tomb. Mark sees the Temple Guard come to stand sentry-go near the tomb, which they seal up. Two days later, Mark wakes at dawn, and sees the Temple Guard, amazed and terrified, running to report to the High Priest that the body of Jesus is no longer in the tomb. Mark rushes to see for himself, and finds the grave-clothes wound round — nothing! Meanwhile, Mary Magdalene and two other women, Mary and Salome, have come to the tomb to embalm the body. They no sooner notice that the tomb is open, when Mark appears from within. The women are afraid, thinking he is a spirit. It is dawn, on the first Easter Day.

STORY BY CHAD VARAH:
DRAWN BY BELLAVITIS.

DON'T BE AFRAID! YOU'RE LOOKING FOR JESUS, WHO WAS CRUCIFIED — THIS *IS* THE PLACE WHERE HE WAS LAID, BUT HE'S NOT HERE — HE'S RISEN!

GO, THEN — BUT TELL HIS FRIENDS HE'LL BE GOING TO GALILEE AS HE TOLD THEM. THEY'LL SEE HIM THERE. TELL PETER TOO!

PITY I STARTLED THEM. IF I GO, P'RAPS THEY'LL COME BACK. I MUST TELL MOTHER, ANYWAY...

At Mark's house...

MARK, WHEREEVER HAVE YOU BEEN? I LOOKED FOR YOU ON THE ROOF, AND...

MOTHER, JESUS IS ALIVE AGAIN!

I'VE BEEN TO THE TOMB. IT'S EMPTY! THE WINDING-SHEET'S THERE, BUT THERE'S NO BODY IN IT — AND *IT COULDN'T HAVE BEEN TAKEN OFF WITH-OUT BEING UNWOUND!*

HE'S RISEN, JUST AS HE SAID!

SO THERE'S NOTHING TO BE AFRAID OF ANY MORE! HE'S CONQUERED DEATH ITSELF! GOD BE PRAISED!

GO AND GET YOUR CLOTHES ON, AND THEN YOU MUST RUN AND TELL *ALL* HIS DISCIPLES TO MEET HERE. AND HAVE A GOOD WASH, MIND!

That evening...

WELCOME, PETER! YOU'RE ALL HERE NOW, I THINK.

EXCEPT THOMAS — I COULDN'T FIND HIM. AND JUDAS, OF COURSE...

AYE, JUDAS — I HAVE AS LITTLE RIGHT TO BE HERE AS HE. BUT MARY MAGDALENE HAS *SEEN* JESUS, AND HE SAID I WAS TO COME.

SEEN HIM?

I MUST HAVE A WORD WITH MAGDALENE. YOU CAN GUARD THE DOOR FOR A WHILE, MARK, BUT DON'T GO IN.

RIGHT, MOTHER.

PEACE BE WITH YOU.

THAT'S — THAT'S JESUS' VOICE!

CONTINUED

The life story of **JOHN MARK,** writer of the 2nd Gospel

Jerusalem, March A.D.29 – the first Easter Day. Jesus has been crucified and buried two days before. So many of the Jewish people loved him and believed he was their promised King that the authorities had had to arrest him secretly. By the time his admirers knew what was happening, it was too late to save him. His disciples, who had run away when he was arrested, were in despair. There was nothing more to do except for the women, who wanted to embalm his body decently. But the tomb was sealed, and watched by the Temple Guard. Mark has woken early, and seeing the Guard running to report to the High Priest that the body has disappeared, goes to the tomb and finds it open and empty except for the graveclothes. The women are startled when Mark emerges from the tomb and run away, so Mark returns and tells his mother that Jesus has risen from the dead. That evening, all the disciples except Thomas and the traitor Judas meet at Mark's house, in the upstairs room, and Peter reports that Mary Magdalene has actually *seen* Jesus. Later, Mark himself hears Jesus's voice through the closed door of the meeting-room!

STORY BY CHAD VARAH : DRAWN BY BELLAVITIS.

PEACE BE WITH YOU.

JESUS!

IT'S THE MASTER!

IS IT A VISION?

I DENIED YOU, LORD!

DON'T BE WORRIED — IT'S REALLY ME! FEEL MY HANDS — GHOSTS DON'T HAVE FLESH AND BONES LIKE THIS! HAVE YOU ANYTHING TO EAT?

THIS PROVES HE'S REAL — IF I'M AWAKE!

HERE'S SOME HONEYCOMB, IF YOU PREFER IT TO THE FISH.

IT'S *REALLY* TRUE! NOT A DREAM, NOT IMAGINATION — THEY CAN SEE AND TOUCH HIM! OH *WHY* DID MUM SAY I MUSTN'T GO IN?

I SEND YOU INTO THE WORLD AS MY FATHER SENT ME. IF *YOU* FORGIVE ANYONE'S SINS, THEY'RE FORGIVEN BY GOD — IF YOU DON'T, THEY ARE NOT FORGIVEN.

I CAME AS SOON AS I HEARD. WHAT'S ALL THIS ABOUT THE MASTER BEING ALIVE?

HE IS! HE'S IN THERE! THOMAS, *DO* LEAVE THE DOOR OPEN...

WHY, HE'S GONE!

WAS NEVER HERE, YOU MEAN. I KNEW IT WAS JUST SILLY WOMEN'S CHATTER. MAGDALENE CRAZED WITH GRIEF, AND...

HE *WAS* HERE, THOMAS. WE ALL SAW HIM. I TOUCHED HIM!

I'LL BELIEVE *THAT* WHEN I SEE THE WOUNDS IN HIS HANDS — AND PUT MY FINGER INTO THE HOLES! ILLUSION, THAT'S WHAT IT IS.

HOW DID HE GET OUT, EH?

SAME WAY HE GOT IN, I SUPPOSE!

THE DOOR WAS SHUT...

I DON'T THINK HE CAME *OR* WENT!

JESUS, I THINK YOU'RE HERE ALL THE TIME! NEXT TIME YOU SHOW YOURSELF, MAY I SEE YOU TOO?

CONTINUED

The life story of
JOHN MARK,
writer of the 2nd Gospel

Jerusalem, the 16th day of the month Nisan (March 20) A.D.29. In one week, Mark's hero – Jesus of Nazareth – has been acclaimed as King of the Jews by the common people, rejected and condemned by the religious authorities, betrayed by one of his twelve chief followers and deserted by the rest, found innocent by the Roman Governor but flogged and crucified nevertheless, and buried in a guarded tomb. Mark and others have now found the tomb empty, and all the disciples except the traitor Judas and Thomas "the Twin" have met in the big upper room at Mark's mother's house. Mark guards the door and hears Jesus's voice from within. The disciples tell Mark and Thomas, who has just arrived, that they have seen *and touched* Jesus – that he is really alive again, not a ghost. Thomas refuses to believe this unless he can see and touch Jesus himself, and asks how did he get out of the room without opening the door? Mark says he is certain that Jesus is there even when they can't actually see him; and, speaking to Jesus, says "Next time, may I see you too?"

STORY BY CHAD VARAH: DRAWN BY BELLAVITIS.

THE LAD HAS MORE FAITH THAN WE HAVE, JOHN.

I SAW THE EMPTY TOMB, PETER.

SO DID WE. BUT WE DIDN'T KNOW WHAT TO THINK UNTIL WE SAW HIM.

HUH!

I KNOW HE WAS HERE. I HEARD HIS VOICE PLAINLY. BUT I *DO* WANT TO SEE HIM.

YOU WILL, MARK.

I WONDER...

...HIS WAYS AREN'T OURS. *WE'D* WANT TO APPEAR TO CAIAPHAS AND PILATE, BUT I DON'T THINK *HE* WILL — HE'LL APPEAR TO CHOSEN WITNESSES...

IF YOU MEAN THE TWELVE, THOMAS WOULD SEE HIM AND I WOULDN'T. IT'S NOT FAIR!

CAN'T YOU SEE YOU'RE THE LUCKY ONE? YOU ALREADY HAVE FAITH, AND NEED NO MORE PROOF.

Next day,

HULLO, CLEOPAS! HULLO, MARY! WHAT ARE YOU DOING IN JERUSALEM? I THOUGHT YOU WENT BACK TO EMMAUS YESTERDAY.

WE DID. BUT WE CAME BACK LAST NIGHT TO TELL THE OTHERS ABOUT SEEING JESUS.

YOU SAW HIM, TOO? AT EMMAUS?

HE WALKED WITH US, AND WE DIDN'T KNOW HIM — DUSK WAS FALLING.

THEN HE CAME IN TO SUPPER, AND AS HE BROKE THE BREAD WE REALIZED — AND HE VANISHED.

I WANT TO KEEP THE PLATTER HE USED — SO I'M BUYING A NEW ONE.

I'M GLAD YOU SAW HIM. IF HE'S APPEARING TO OTHERS BESIDES THE TWELVE, THERE'S A CHANCE FOR ME!

The next Sunday.

HURRY UP, MARK. YOU'RE SUPPOSED TO BE GUARDING THE DOOR UPSTAIRS.

I'M JUST FINISHING MY SUPPER, MOTHER.

FEEL THE WOUNDS IN MY HANDS AND SIDE, THOMAS! DON'T BE FAITHLESS, BUT BELIEVE THE TRUTH!

Meanwhile, upstairs...

YOU'RE MY LORD AND MY GOD!

MOTHER DIDN'T FORBID ME TO GO IN THIS TIME — SO IF HE'S THERE, I'LL SEE HIM!

CONTINUED

The life story of JOHN MARK, writer of the 2nd Gospel

Jerusalem, Sunday 27th March A.D.29. It is ten days since Jesus of Nazareth was crucified, and buried in a sealed and guarded tomb; and a week since he rose from the dead and appeared to his mother, to Mary Magdalene, to Peter and the rest of the Eleven except Thomas. Mark, who was the first (except for the guards) to explore the empty tomb, is longing to see Jesus, especially since talking to Cleopas and his wife Mary, with whom Jesus walked on the road to Emmaus, for they were "ordinary" disciples like Mark himself. When guarding the door of the Upper Room in his mother's house, Mark had heard the voice of the risen Jesus within, and believes that he is near all the time, even when invisible. Now all the Apostles, including Thomas, are in the Upper Room, and Jesus is there speaking to Thomas, who doubted the Resurrection, as Mark arrives late to guard the door -- for Jesus's friends are still in danger of arrest. Mark determines to go in and see Jesus for himself, if he hears his voice.

STORY BY CHAD VARAH : DRAWN BY BELLAVITIS.

THOMAS, YOU NOW BELIEVE I'M ALIVE, BECAUSE YOU'VE SEEN ME.

JESUS'S VOICE! HE'S THERE! I'LL KNOCK AND GO IN QUICKLY...

BLESSED ARE THOSE WHO CAN BELIEVE *WITHOUT* HAVING SEEN ME!

HE MEANT *ME* — NOT *ONLY* ME, OF COURSE, BUT— HE KNOWS I'M HERE, AND HE KNOWS I BELIEVE HE'S REALLY ALIVE...

IT'S DISAPPOINTING, BUT I MUST DO AS *HE* WANTS. PERHAPS IF I'M PATIENT...

I SAY, MARK!

WE'RE TO GO TO A CERTAIN MOUNTAIN IN GALILEE TO MEET JESUS. IF YOU LIKE, I'LL ASK YOUR MOTHER IF YOU CAN COME WITH US.

OH, *PETER!*

A hilltop in Galilee.

TEACH AND BAPTIZE ALL NATIONS— I'LL ALWAYS BE WITH YOU, TILL THE WORLD ENDS.

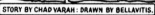

ORTY days after Easter Day, Jesus took the eleven Apostles up the Mount of Olives, told them to wait in Jerusalem until the power of the Holy Spirit came into them, and said Good-bye. He ascended into heaven, and they knew they wouldn't see him on earth again. Ten days later, at the Jewish Harvest Festival ("Pentecost") the Spirit came upon the disciples.

Pentecost (Whitsun) evening.

YOU MUST BE TIRED AFTER YOUR BUSY DAY.

NOT A BIT, MARY. BUT IT *WAS* BUSY. THREE THOUSAND BAPTIZED!

AT THIS RATE, THE WHOLE WORLD WILL SOON BE DISCIPLES OF JESUS.

IT WILL BE HARDER FOR THE PEOPLE WHO AREN'T JEWS TO BELIEVE IN HIM. THEY DON'T KNOW GOD AT ALL.

MOTHER, WHEN PETER AND JOHN GO ABROAD TO PREACH, MAY I GO WITH THEM? I'VE BEEN PRACTISING HERE IN JERUSALEM.

YOU MUSTN'T DO THAT!

WHY EVER NOT?

IT'S DANGEROUS!

IT'S NO WORK FOR BOYS. I'M EXPECTING TO BE ARRESTED ANY DAY.

BUT YOU'RE NOT AFRAID — AND NEITHER AM I! WELL, NOT MUCH — I KNOW JESUS IS GOD, AND I SHALL GO ON TELLING EVERYBODY SO!

CONTINUED

The life story of
JOHN MARK,
writer of the 2nd Gospel

Jerusalem, Whitsun evening, A.D.29. It is 50 days since Jesus rose from the dead and was seen alive by over 500 people, including Mark. It is ten days since Jesus returned to Heaven, and the Holy Spirit he promised to send to guide and strengthen his friends has come. The disciples who deserted their Master to save their own skins are now full of the courage of Jesus himself, and in one day have converted and baptized 3,000 people, Jews like themselves. Now Peter and John are having supper at the house of Mary, Mark's mother. Mark wants to preach the faith of Christ too, and remarks that he has been practising in Jerusalem already. His mother, knowing well that Peter is likely to be arrested any day, says that the work is far too dangerous for a boy. Mark replies that he knows Jesus is God and will go on telling everyone so!

YOU SHOULDN'T DEFY YOUR MOTHER, MARK! REMEMBER THE COMMANDMENT!

JESUS SAID LOVE OF GOD MUST COME EVEN BEFORE LOVE OF PARENTS.

I'M SORRY I WAS RUDE, MOTHER. JESUS *DID* TELL US TO BEAR WITNESS...

YES, AND WE MUST OBEY HIM WITHOUT FEAR.

STORY BY CHAD VARAH: DRAWN BY BELLAVITIS.

YOU KNOW, MOTHER— ALL BOYS WANT ADVENTURE...

MOTHERS EASILY GET ANXIOUS. BE A BIT CAREFUL FOR MY SAKE, DEAR.

Next day.

I ADMIT THE TOMB'S EMPTY. THE BODY'S BEEN MOVED. BUT CORPSES DON'T MOVE THEMSELVES!

PLEASE, SIR, WHO MOVED IT?

HIS FRIENDS, OF COURSE — SO THAT THEY COULD PRETEND HE'D "RISEN".

I DON'T BELIEVE *THAT.*

THE TOMB WAS GUARDED. BESIDES, I'VE LISTENED TO THOSE MEN. I DON'T BELIEVE WHAT THEY SAY, BUT I'D SWEAR *THEY* BELIEVE IT.

YOU'RE RIGHT, SIR — SOMETHING HAS MADE THOSE MEN BRAVE. DECEIT WOULDN'T DO THAT.

ATTENTION, *PLEASE!* I'M GOING TO LET YOU INTO THE SECRET!

THE HIGH PRIEST HAS THE BODY HIDDEN AWAY.

IF HE HAD, HE'D PRODUCE IT.

AYE—IT'D MAKE THOSE DISCIPLES LOOK SILLY, AND SETTLE THE MATTER.

I'M SICK OF YOUR INTERFERENCE — BE OFF WITH YOU, OR I'LL HAVE YOU ARRESTED!

OH !

NOW, AS I WAS SAYING...

YOU BIG BULLY! HITTING THE LAD BECAUSE HE WAS TOO CLEVER FOR YOU!

BOYS SHOULD BE SEEN AND NOT HEARD.

HE'S A PAID AGENT OF CAIAPHAS! HE'S TOLD YOU TWO DIFFERENT STORIES — BOTH LIES!

YOU'LL BE SORRY FOR THIS!

THE TRUTH IS, THAT JESUS IS ALIVE — I SAW HIM WITH MY OWN EYES, BEFORE HE WENT BACK TO HEAVEN! BELIEVE AND BE BAPTIZED!

YOU WAIT! I'LL GET YOU ONE DAY, IF IT'S THE LAST THING I DO!

CONTINUED

The life story of
JOHN MARK,
writer of the 2nd Gospel

Jerusalem, A.D.29. The day after the founding of the Christian Church on the first Whitsun Day, Mark, excited by the conversion of 3,000 Jews in one day, is determined to imitate Peter and John and the other Apostles in preaching that Jesus's Resurrection proves that he really is the Christ, the Divine King sent by God. Near the City wall, he heckles an agent of the High Priest who first says that Jesus's tomb was empty because the disciples stole the body, and later that Caiaphas has the body concealed. Mark earns himself a clip on the head, but climbs up the wall where the agent can't follow, and tells the crowd he himself saw the Risen Christ. The agent, infuriated by the interruptions, threatens to 'get' Mark, if it's the last thing he does!

STORY BY CHAD VARAH: DRAWN BY BELLAVITIS.

I'M NOT AFRAID OF YOU! WE CHRISTIANS AREN'T AFRAID OF *ANYTHING* NOW!

YOU'LL CHANGE YOUR TUNE WHEN WE CATCH YOU!

EVEN IF YOU KILL US, IT ONLY MEANS WE GO TO HIM. WE'D RATHER DIE THAN SAVE OUR LIVES BY DENYING HIM!

STOP THAT BOY! FETCH THE TEMPLE GUARD, SOMEONE!

YOU CAN'T CATCH *ME*!

YON'S A BRAVE LAD— AND A CLEVER LAD— EVEN IF HE *IS* A BIT CHEEKY.

DON'T TELL ANYONE, BUT— I'M BEGINNING TO THINK WHAT HE SAYS IS TRUE!

OH, NO YOU'RE NOT! IF YOU BELIEVED IT, YOU'D HAVE THE SAME GUTS AS THAT LAD, INSTEAD OF WHINING "DON'T TELL ANYONE".

I—I ONLY MEANT...

YOU MEANT YOU WANT TO SIT ON THE FENCE. WITH JESUS, IT'S ALL OR NOTHING. OH, IF ONLY I WAS A MAN, I'D SHOW 'EM!

THERE HE GOES, BEHIND THAT HOUSE! ONE OF YOU GET UP EACH SIDE AND CLOSE IN ON HIM! QUICK!

RIGHT, SIR!

THEY'VE SEEN ME! WHICHEVER WAY I GO, THEY'LL CUT ME OFF. I'M TRAPPED!

I MUST GET AWAY IF I CAN. NO USE *ASKING* FOR TROUBLE! IF I CAN SNEAK DOWN THROUGH THE HOUSE...

THAT'S FUNNY — NO SIGN OF HIM. HE MUST HAVE RUN PRETTY QUICKLY...

GOT YOU! WHAT ARE YOU DOING IN OUR HOUSE?

LET ME GO— I'M A DISCIPLE OF JESUS, AND THE TEMPLE GUARD ARE AFTER ME!

LET YOU GO? NOT LIKELY! THERE'LL BE A GOOD REWARD FOR HANDING YOU OVER TO THE AUTHORITIES!

CONTINUED

The life story of
JOHN MARK,
writer of the 2nd Gospel

Jerusalem, Whit Monday, A.D.29. Inspired by the gift of the Holy Spirit the previous day, Peter and the other Apostles have converted 3,000 people to belief in the Risen Christ. Mark is determined to play his part in building up the new Christian Church, and heckles an agent of the High Priest so effectively that the man calls the Temple Guard to arrest the boy. Mark's words have made a great impression on two people in the crowd, but he is too busy trying to escape to follow them up. Trapped by two Guards on the City wall, he climbs on to the roof of a nearby house and down through a trapdoor — only to be seized by a bigger boy who hopes to receive a reward for handing him over!

STORY BY CHAD VARAH: DRAWN BY BELLAVITIS.

ALL RIGHT — HAND ME OVER, AND GET YOUR REWARD. IT WON'T DO YOU ANY GOOD, AND I'M NOT AFRAID.

JACOB! WHAT'S GOING ON HERE?

CAUGHT THIS LAD COMING FROM THE ROOF — THOUGHT HE WAS A THIEF, BUT HE'S WANTED BY THE TEMPLE GUARD. THERE'LL BE A REWARD, MOTHER...

OH, NO THERE WON'T!

I'VE BEEN LISTENING TO THE LAD, DOWN BY THE GATE. HE'S CONVINCED *ME* THAT JESUS REALLY ROSE FROM THE DEAD.

BUT THE MONEY, MOTHER! WE NEED IT!

NOT THAT SORT OF MONEY, WE DON'T! HE'S TAUGHT ME THAT JESUS IS GOD'S CHRIST, AND I SHALL LET HIM GO.

IF YOU DO, I'LL SPLIT ON YOU — AND *YOU'LL* BE IN TROUBLE TOO!

A FINE SON YOU ARE! ALL RIGHT — IT MIGHT AS WELL BE NOW AS LATER. I'VE MADE UP MY MIND TO BE BAPTIZED, AND JOIN THE CHRISTIANS.

HAND ME OVER AND CLAIM YOUR REWARD — BUT DON'T BETRAY YOUR OWN MOTHER.

I WASN'T GOING TO! I WAS JUST MAD BECAUSE SHE LET YOU GO — YOU'RE MY PRISONER.

COME ON, THEN. I PROMISE YOU I WON'T TRY TO ESCAPE.

ER — DON'T BE IN SUCH A HURRY...

...YOU'VE GOT GUTS, I MUST SAY. I'VE NEVER BEEN MUCH FOR RELIGION MYSELF — WHAT'S IT ALL ABOUT? WHO'S THIS MAN JESUS YOU'RE READY TO DIE FOR?

I'LL TELL YOU...

THERE'S NO OTHER EXPLANATION. HE MUST'VE GOT INTO THIS HOUSE VIA THE ROOF.

THEN WE'VE GOT HIM. YOU KEEP WATCH WHILE I SEARCH EVERY ROOM.

A few minutes later.

GOT HIM! COME AND — GIVE ME — A HAND...

I'LL SOON SETTLE THE LITTLE BLIGHTER!

HE FOUGHT LIKE A TIGER!

THERE'LL BE NO MORE TROUBLE FROM HIM NOW! WAIT TILL HE COMES ROUND — WE DON'T WANT TO HAVE TO CARRY HIM TO HEADQUARTERS!

CONTINUED

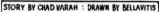

The life story of JOHN MARK, writer of the 2nd Gospel

Jerusalem, Whit Monday, A.D.29. Mark is determined to play his part in building up the Christian Church, founded by the Holy Spirit the previous day, and already numbering 3,000 – all Jews. Temple Guards are called to arrest him after he has heckled an agent of the High Priest who was denying Jesus' Resurrection. Mark escapes through the roof of a house near the city wall, only to be seized by a bigger boy who sees a chance of a reward. But the boy's mother has been convinced by Mark's arguments, and challenges her son to hand *her* over to the Guards, too. Meanwhile, two Guards come to search the house for young Mark, and after a violent struggle with a boy who is trying to leave, they knock him out, and wait for him to recover consciousness so that he can walk with them to their headquarters.

STORY BY CHAD VARAH : DRAWN BY BELLAVITIS

EXCUSE ME, GIRL — HAVE YOU SEEN ANY OF THE TEMPLE GUARD AROUND?

YES, SIR — TWO OF THE BRAVE FELLOWS WERE FIGHTING A BOY. LOOK, THERE'S ONE OF THEM!

GOOD — HE DIDN'T RECOGNIZE ME. HOPE THEY DON'T HURT JACOB . . . I MUST GO HOME AND CHANGE MY CLOTHES...

GLAD YOU'VE COME, SIR. WE'VE GOT THE BOY, BUT HIS MOTHER'S CREATING AN AWFUL FUSS — SAYS HE HASN'T BEEN OUT ALL DAY !

LET ME SEE HIM !

YOU'LL BE ABLE TO PROVE IT, SIR ! I WAS IN THE CROWD WHEN THAT LAD INTERRUPTED YOU — MY BOY'S NOT A BIT LIKE HIM !

I REMEMBER YOU.

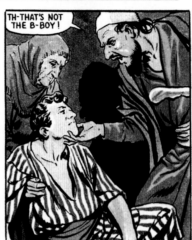

TH-THAT'S NOT THE B-BOY !

I MUST APOLOGIZE FOR THOSE IDIOTS, MADAM, BUT . . . HEY, THAT'S FISHY ! YOUR BOY'S WEARING THE SAME CLOTHES !

OH, YOU MEN ! HALF THE BOYS IN JERUS-ALEM WEAR THE SAME !

That evening . . .

HUNDREDS MORE CONVERTS TO-DAY. NO WONDER YOU'RE TIRED, PETER.

I WISH MARK WOULD COME. I'M NERVOUS AFTER HIS NARROW ESCAPE FROM ARREST...

HERE HE COMES NOW — AND IT LOOKS AS IF HE'S HAD GREAT SUCCESS !

THREE NEW CHRISTIANS, PETER !

WELCOME, BROTHERS — WELCOME, SISTER. WELL DONE, MARK !

DO YOU BELIEVE IN JESUS CHRIST, THE SON OF GOD, YOUR RISEN SAVIOUR?

YES, YES — I'M QUITE CONVINCED.

YES, SIR, I DO.

AYE.

NOW MAY I BE A MISSIONARY, PETER?

YES, MARK. YOU SHALL WORK WITH ME. AND REMEMBER — NOT EVEN DEATH WILL END OUR GREAT ADVENTURE!

Mark's further adventures are part of Peter's story, which we hope to tell you some time.